YOSEMITE AS WE SAW IT

HINSHELWOOD AND HILL
*Yosemite Valley*, no date
Chromolithograph
Courtesy, Bancroft Library

# YOSEMITE AS WE SAW IT

## A CENTENNIAL COLLECTION
## OF EARLY WRITINGS AND ART

*David Robertson*

*assisted by*

*Henry Berrey*

*Foreword by*

*Kevin Starr*

YOSEMITE ASSOCIATION

1990

*for Ellen, Karen, and Joan*
*and*
*Timothy, Henry IV, Thomas, and Allen*

Yosemite Association
P.O. Box 545
Yosemite National Park, CA 95389

The Yosemite Association is a non-profit, membership organization dedicated to the support of Yosemite National Park. Our publishing program is designed to provide an educational service and to increase the public's understanding of Yosemite's special qualities and needs. To learn more about our activities and other publications, or for information about membership, please write to the address above, or call (209) 379-2646.

LIBRARY OF CONGRESS CATALOGING-IN-PUBLICATION DATA
Robertson, David, 1937-
Yosemite as we saw it: a centennial collection of early writings and art / by David Robertson; assisted by Henry Berrey.
Bibliographic index: pp. 97-100
1. Yosemite National Park (Calif.) 2. Yosemite National Park (Calif.) in art. I. Title.
F868.Y6R58 1990
979.4'47—dc20
89-28251 CIP

ISBN 0-939666-53-7

Cover:
LOUIS PRANG
*Yosemite Valley*, ca. 1869
Chromolithograph after a painting by Thomas Hill
Courtesy, Boston Public Library

# CONTENTS

# LIST OF ILLUSTRATIONS

# ACKNOWLEDGMENTS

MANY PEOPLE have helped us research and write this book. Most important are the personnel of the National Park Service in Yosemite: Dave Forgang and Barbara Beroza in the Collection Room; Mary Vocelka and Linda Eade in the Research Library; Leonard McKenzie, Chief Park Interpreter; Jim Snyder, Park Historian; and Jack Morehead, Park Superintendent. A number of additional people associated with the Park also contributed to our efforts: Virginia Adams; Jeanne Adams, President of the Ansel Adams Gallery; and Robert Woolard, who made transparencies and prints of material in the Yosemite Collection. Our thanks also go to the staff of the Bancroft Library at the University of California, Berkeley, who patiently retrieved volume after volume from its archives, as well as to various individuals at the California Historical Society, the Oakland Museum, and the Boston Public Library. A special thanks goes to Steve Medley, President of the Yosemite Association, and to his extraordinarily competent staff. In addition, we want to thank the Members of the Board of Trustees of the Yosemite Association, who entrusted us with this project. Finally, we want to say a heartfelt thank you to our wives, Jeannette and Eileen.

C. CRANE
*The Valley of the Yosemite*, 1874
From *America Illustrated*, edited by J. David Williams
Boston: DeWolfe, Fiske & Co., 1883, page 67
Yosemite Collection

# FOREWORD

OVER THE YEARS, certain places have become occasions and premises for the process of self-identification among the American people. For early nineteenth-century Americans, Niagara Falls embodied the power and grandeur of the American continent and the possibilities of the newly enfranchised Republic. In the mid-nineteenth-century era, wracked by a sectional division that only a terrible civil war could subdue, the mighty Mississippi, running down the center of the continent, functioned as a symbolic spinal cord conferring life and unity upon a traumatized body politic.

In the second half of the nineteenth century, as this *sui generis* anthology asserts so powerfully, the Yosemite emerged in the national imagination as an icon of identity fully equal to Niagara and the Mississippi. The very rollcall of writers represented in this analytical assembly of responses testifies to the national, indeed international, hold exercised by the Yosemite on the American and European imaginations. We encounter such visiting Eastern journalists as Horace Greeley and Samuel Bowles. Well-known travel writers from the era are represented by, among others, Fitz Hugh Ludlow, Sara Jane Lippincott, and Helen Hunt Jackson. There are the Eastern scientists sojourning in the West, Yale-trained geologists many of them, such as Josiah Whitney and Clarence King; and the resident California intellectuals and litterateurs from the High Provincial Era (to borrow Josiah Royce's term): the Unitarian-Universalist minister Thomas Starr King of San Francisco, for example, the educator Ezra Carr, poet Charles Warren Stoddard, and another parson (albeit defrocked), George Wharton James, a ceaseless writer on behalf of California's emergent culture. The Big Three of Yosemite literature—James Mason Hutchings, Joseph LeConte, and John Muir, the greatest of them all—are more than adequately represented. The accounts of LeConte's death in the Yosemite and the funeral procession of his rough-hewn coffin filled with pine boughs is especially compelling. All in all, David Robertson has drawn upon more than ninety primary statements, ranging from acknowledged literary classics to diaries only recently excavated from the archives.

*Yosemite As We Saw It* is a distinctive form of book, a hybrid between an anthology and an analytical monograph. As the acknowledged expert on the symbolic significance of Yosemite in American culture, Professor Robertson is carrying on two tasks simultaneously. First of all, he has read and selected the most revealing literary responses to the Yosemite down through the nineteenth and early twentieth centuries, with the poet Gary Snyder hammering a piton into the present. *Yosemite As We Saw It* thus functions as the most comprehensive anthology of Yosemite literature ever to be made available to the public. Strictly in these terms, as a gathering of significant voices and statements, this book succeeds and satisfies.

But Robertson has done more than merely select and annotate. He has analyzed, categorized, and thematically linked these literary responses. *Yosemite As We Saw It* presents the reader with the structure and semiotics of the nineteenth- and early twentieth-century American experience of the Yosemite. With great skill, Robertson isolates and decodes the cumulative meaning accruing from the texts extending over a century. The most apparent principle of organization comes from the Yosemite environment itself. For more than thirteen decades, Americans have entered the Yosemite Valley on more or less the same route, beheld the same monoliths, waterfalls, cliffs, and trees—and exited along a correspondingly similar route and with a correspondingly similar cluster of psychological and imaginative responses.

For the first time, however, Robertson also presents the more subtly existential, frequently fearful, and sometimes even darker aspects of the Yosemite encounter. Sublime and majestic, the Yosemite inspired more than its share of thrilled responses. But the very force of the valley, its trans-human sublimity and scale, could also provoke feelings of inadequacy, even dread, in early visitors. The very force of nature, after all, stood so grandly manifest in the Yosemite that some visitors found themselves fearful, as if they could suddenly feel the planet turn on its axis or hurtle through space. An earthquake provokes this same terror as we feel the full force of the planet which nature so mercifully hides from us most of the time. Nineteenth-century geologists were enamored of catastrophism: the belief that formations such as the Yosemite were caused by sudden and abrupt transformations. From this perspective, the Yosemite could seem, not an eternal achievement, but a temporary balance of energies and forces, capable of continuing its catastrophic evolution in a split second. Thus the Yosemite could frequently seem a precarious instant of quietude and repose between the cosmic upheaval that had once been and could at any second continue to unfold.

Fortunately, this dread of the sheer force of nature as revealed in the Yosemite, as Robertson presents it through selection and analysis, was offset by more persistently optimistic responses. As *Yosemite As We Saw It* asserts so amply, the great valley soothed and reconciled its visitors more than it intimidated them. Again, however, Robertson presents us with a complexity of levels of response. Not only did Americans find the Yosemite sublime and beautiful, they found in its majesty an existential encounter that led to renewal and affirmation. In the case of John Muir, prophet and avatar of all that the Yosemite offered, the valley brought him to an intuitive communion with the very essence of creation itself: a comprehension of nature as a whole and a personal conviction that his place in nature was assured and holy.

In this religious dimension Robertson, a trained theologian as well as a literary scholar, shows a unique sensitivity. The notion that nature was a direct emanation of the mind of God haunted Americans since the theologizing of Jonathan Edwards in the mid-eighteenth century. Thomas Starr King was the first to bring this sensibility to the Yosemite itself. King read the valley as a sermonic text comparable to scripture. Even in our own less-believing or belief-embattled age, the Yosemite still engenders in the majority of Americans a feeling of reverence and awe (Sigmund Freud called it the Oceanic Feeling) that is the psychological matrix for all quests for transcendence through religion or philosophy. Even natural religion creeps slyly into *Yosemite As We Saw It* in the personifications imposed upon the great monoliths. From this perspective, Half Dome and El Capitan rose from the valley floor—not just in the imaginations of Native Americans but in the minds of subsequent visitors as well—like great totem gods, personified and mysteriously alive, like the statues on Easter Island. The most refined perceptions of religious experience, Robertson realizes and elegantly documents, build on mytho-poetic formulations that take us back to the beginnings of the human race and mankind's first clumsy efforts to make sense of the universe.

One hundred years ago the Yosemite was set aside as a national park. Even before this designation, however, the Yosemite had been fixed at the center of the American national imagination, having long since become one of those symbolic places through which Americans identified themselves and all the possibilities of the continent they inhabited. Published for the centennial year, *Yosemite As We Saw It* celebrates more than 130 years of American encounter with the Yosemite, together with the thousands of years of Native American responses. And back behind that is an infinity of time extending to the very creation of the valley itself.

Unlike some nineteenth-century visitors, we need not fear that the Yosemite will overwhelm us. On the contrary, modern technologies and lifestyles have made it fully possible for us to overwhelm the Yosemite: to use it up through heedless recreation. As grand and compelling as the Yosemite is as a geological phenomenon and a symbol in our collective imagination, it is nevertheless a parcel of the environment and hence liable to damage from human misuse. *Yosemite As We Saw It* serves therefore as a challenge and a warning. A century hence another anthology of comparable responses might very well be assembled. One hopes that such an anthology will record the growing presence and power of the transforming, salvific aspects of Yosemite's meaning in the American experience and imagination. If so, if all goes well, that is, this future anthology will chronicle the fact that throughout the twenty-first century visitors from around the world came to the Yosemite as did their counterparts two hundred years earlier. They came to it and they felt its power. They cherished its meaning, and they left the valley with the renewed sense that nature is part of us and we are part of nature, and in that point of connection between valley and person, place and symbolic power, we can touch the deepest mysteries of humanity and its brief sojourn on this planet.

KEVIN STARR

HARRY CASSIE BEST
*Yosemite Valley from Inspiration Point*, no date
Oil on canvas
Yosemite Collection

# INTRODUCTION

THE QUINTESSENTIAL YOSEMITE EXPERIENCE has two phases. Being overwhelmed comes first. A series of massive shapes and delicate lines arranged in deep space on an inconceivably grand harmonic scale surrounds you and leaves you speechless. Merging with this engulfing landscape dissolves the sense that you are separate from your environment. You belong not only to this particular place, this Yosemite, but also, in a strange and mystical way, to the whole of Nature. An abiding peace moves through you and out to the farthest reaches of the universe.

So overpowering is Yosemite that people have recognized the need for a radical reorientation of thought and feeling in order to comprehend it:

> Upon our first view of El Capitan, as we were walking into the valley, one bright July forenoon, we stopped a mile and a half from its foot, collected ourselves for a calm, cool, mathematical judgment and said with all confidence, "That rock isn't over fifteen hundred feet high. It *can't* be. Why just look at that tree near its base. That tree, certainly, can't be more than a hundred and twenty-five feet high, and certainly, the cliff doesn't rise more than ten times its height above it." But, unfortunately, we had forgotten that never before had we seen the works of nature on as grand a scale. One's judgment has to change its base. He has to reconstruct it; to adopt a new unit. Comparison serves him little, for he has no adequate standard by which to measure, or with which to compare the rock-mountains before him. They are like nothing else. They are a law unto themselves, and one must learn the law, the *new* law, before he can begin to enter the secret of their greatness. [*Bancroft's Tourist's Guide (1871) 50.*]

In the early days most people were overwhelmed upon first seeing the Yosemite panorama from the old trails that led into the valley from the west. Once the Yosemite word was out, however, advance publicity sometimes raised expectations too high. In those cases, the initial response was disappointment. It took a few days and a more intimate knowledge of the land for the spell to take effect. Nowadays, packaged tours and packed schedules promote the casual glance. But the visionary experience is still available, and always will be, to those who open their eyes and let the spirit within them see.

Because first sight of Yosemite so often leaves people at a loss for words, they usually begin narratives of their adventures in the park with a lamentation: Woe is me, I have promised to describe this place for you, but I cannot:

> Any attempt to describe the unutterable grandeur and sublimity of the scene only serves to demonstrate the pitiful inadequacy of our language to measure up to such a task. It is utterly beyond the power of language to convey any impression of the awe-inspiring majesty of the walls of solid granite that enclose the Valley on every side. [*Herbert Earl Wilson*, THE LORE AND THE LURE OF YOSEMITE *(1928) 32.*]

Perhaps pictures give a more accurate impression of the place. People frequently believe pictures, especially photographs, when they distrust words. Yet visual artists of Yosemite also bemoan their plight:

> To describe Yosemite's light in its mellowness, its refreshing sensation of color-coolness upon the eye, and of contented and dreamy languor upon the mind, is to approach so closely to the confines of the impossible that I, for one, forbear. [*Charles Dorman Robinson, "Painting a Yosemite Panorama" (1893) 246.*]

The basic message is clear: neither verbal nor visual representations do Yosemite justice. You must see it for yourself:

> In trying to put into words the transcendent glories of this land of enchantment, one may, with the help of the camera, produce a counterfeit presentment, more or less satisfying, of heights and depths. But the overlying fascination is beyond the power of language or the genius of the paint brush. It is ethereal, intangible. To the seeing eye alone and to its responsive chord will Yosemite be known in its sublimest and most glorious reality. [*O. W. Lehmer*, YOSEMITE NATIONAL PARK *(1912).*]

Having listened to people assert that Yosemite is beyond description, one might expect them to pack up their pens and paints and rest content with being spellbound. But at this point they enter phase two. The ecstasy is over, and a sense of personal identity precipitates out of the feeling of oneness with the world. As the light of common day dawns once again, they have a need to explain, in terms of common sense, what has just happened to them. So, in spite of all the disclaimers, attempts at description begin.

Invariably one strategy writers adopt is measurement. They list in tables the height of waterfalls, the volume of granite domes, the girth of trees. In the texts that accompany these charts they compare Yosemite phenomena with objects familiar to their readers, like Niagara Falls and the

Empire State Building. Another ploy is to quote Scripture, or a favorite poet, or a recognized authority, such as J. D. Whitney or John Muir.

These strategies, while helpful, are not entirely satisfying. People resort in the end, in spite of a firm belief that their efforts are doomed to mediocrity, to making up words of their own, drawing their own pictures, and printing their own photographic images. That is, they create original art of Yosemite. This has been and probably always will be the most effective method of transcribing Yosemite experiences. Those experiences are, at the deepest level, inituitive and emotional, and art, among all the products of human culture, most depends upon intuition for its genesis. It speaks most directly to the emotions.

But more than transcription is involved here. Yosemite is a huge and mighty Presence on the earth's surface, alive with power. Human beings want not only to feel that presence but also to appropriate for themselves its indwelling power. Yosemite is like the sun: the fusion within it of elementary granite and water radiates light and heat abroad. Art, like solar panels, absorbs the radiation and converts it to forms of emotional and spiritual energy that people can use.

The word niche, as ecologists use the term, has a twofold meaning. It is an organism's address, the territory it occupies within an ecosystem. The main California address of the organism *Homo sapiens* is metropolitan, although it also inhabits towns, farms, and the hill country. In these places people make a complex physical living. They grow and distribute food, build houses and offices, get goods in exchange for currency, dispose of wastes, multiply their kind, and bury their dead.

If, however, we change the frame of reference from the physical to the emotional, it is clear that many people have, over the past 130 years, moved to a new address in the state: Yosemite National Park. Here they have discovered a spiritual niche for themselves, and the migration is on. The magnitude of this migration and the intensity of the feelings evoked suggest that the traditional view of human beings as an exotic species in Yosemite is no longer adequate. They have become genuine, albeit fledgling, members of its natural ecological community. Habitation of Yosemite is not so much an escape from an urban environment as it is an expansion of the human niche in this part of North America. Perhaps people should be called "cohabitants" of Yosemite instead of "visitors." (See Charles C. Rombold, *The National Park Experience* [1981].)

Niche also refers to an organism's occupation, what it does to make a living at its address. Bees, for example, make honey for themselves by visiting flowering plants and returning to the hive laden with pollen. Correspondingly, people visit Yosemite to make an emotional living. While there they gather the kind of pollen that will sustain and expand the human spirit.

Human beings track nourishment in Yosemite almost exclusively by sight. Sound plays a role occasionally, and the sense of smell, so effective for other animals, is hardly ever used. Views and vistas are what these hunters are after. Once they have discovered a site, they use, as do the other animals, mouths and hands to cook and eat. They talk about what they have seen, write it down, draw it, open a shutter on it. Art is culinary technology: landscape is nature raw; a poem, a painting, or a photograph is nature cooked. The purpose of Yosemite art is to make the park digestible by the human emotional tract.

Yosemite As We Saw It is a many-paged banquet of Yosemite art, emphasizing the decades before and after 1890, the year that Yosemite became a national park. The aim of the editors is to let artists serve their own specialties as they prepared them. We have added few seasonings of our own, although we have occasionally cut off some unwanted fat. We have also provided a narrative line and offered commentary here and there. Diarists, travel writers, essayists, poets, photographers, painters, and other graphic artists are included in the bill of fare, amateur as well as professional. The initial chapter mostly presents the thoughts and feelings of the uninitiated at the moment of their induction into glory. The last chapter contains an account of one particularly moving exit from the Park and provides, as well, an occasion for Yosemite veterans to reflect on its lasting meaning and value. In between are chapters on its major features: domes, waterfalls, and big trees. We hope readers will be seated at this table we have spread, eat heartily, and come away emotionally full.

D.R.
H.B.

Kurz and Allison
*Yosemite Water Falls*, no date
Chromolithograph
Courtesy, Bancroft Library

THOMAS AYRES
*The Ford, Entrance to the Yohemity Valley, California,* 1855
Black chalk on charcoal drawing on white paper
Yosemite Collection

# $\mathbb{I}$   ENTRANCES

## *Five Classic Entrances*

FIVE HISTORIC JOURNEYS INTO YOSEMITE VALLEY took place in the middle decades of the nineteenth century. The earliest came in 1851 when the Mariposa Battalion, one of whose members was Lafayette Houghton Bunnell, entered the valley on a punitive mission against the Miwok Indians. Later in the same decade James Hutchings, an Englishman by birth and an overland 49er by choice, made two trips to Yosemite, in 1855 accompanied by the artist Thomas Ayres and in 1859 when the photographer Charles Weed joined his party. In the summer of 1863 the painter Albert Bierstadt and the writer Fitz Hugh Ludlow reached Yosemite at the end of a transcontinental expedition. The last of the five came in 1869 when John Muir, who had sipped from the Yosemite cup the previous year, returned for a summer-long draught.

The narratives of these five entrances are classic accounts of the Yosemite experience: the incomparable grandeur, the mystic ecstasy, the hopeless inadequacy of language, the struggle nevertheless to find metaphors that might measure the height of mountains and the depth of personal feelings, and a strange sense of peace so pervasive that even death loses its sting.

### *Discovery of Yosemite Valley by the Mariposa Battalion in 1851*

On March 27, 1851, a detachment of the Mariposa Battalion, with James D. Savage in command, entered Yosemite Valley in order to remove its native inhabitants to a reservation on the Fresno River. Lafayette Houghton Bunnell, a native New Yorker, had arrived in California in 1849 and was in Mariposa County in time to join Savage's Battalion as its surgeon. Almost thirty years later, in 1880, he published his version of the Battalion's short but momentous history in *Discovery of the Yosemite, and the Indian War of 1851 Which Led to That Event*. The soldiers left Wawona early in the morning and followed the principal Indian trail to the valley. This route crossed the mountains high above the present Wawona road and met the south rim at the place now called Old Inspiration Point:

> We suddenly came in full view of the valley in which was the village, or rather the encampments of the Yosemites. The immensity of rock I had seen in my vision on the Old Bear Valley trail from Ridley's Ferry was here presented to my astonished gaze. My awe was increased by this nearer view.

The face of the immense cliff was shadowed by the declining sun; its outlines only had been seen at a distance. This towering mass

> *"Fools our fond gaze, and greatest of the great,*
> *Defies at first our Nature's littleness,*
> *Till, growing with (to) its growth, we thus dilate*
> *Our spirits to the size of that they contemplate."*

That stupendous cliff is now known as "El Capitan" (the Captain), and the plateau from which we had our first view of the valley, as Mount Beatitude [a rock ledge near Old Inspiration Point].

It has been said that "it is not easy to describe in words the precise impressions which great objects make upon us." I cannot describe how completely I realized this truth. None but those who have visited this most wonderful valley can even imagine the feelings with which I looked upon the view that was there presented. The grandeur of the scene was but softened by the haze that hung over the valley—light as gossamer—and by the clouds which partially dimmed the higher cliffs and mountains. This obscurity of vision but increased the awe with which I beheld it, and as I looked, a peculiar exalted sensation seemed to fill my whole being, and I found my eyes in tears with emotion.

During my subsequent visits to this locality, this sensation was never again so fully aroused. It is probable that the shadows fast clothing all before me, and the vapory clouds at the head of the valley, leaving the view beyond still undefined, gave a weirdness to the scene, that made it so impressive; and the conviction that it was utterly indescribable added strength to the emotion.

To obtain a more distinct and *quiet* view, I had left the trail and my horse and wallowed through the snow alone to a projecting granite rock. So interested was I in the scene before me, that I did not observe that my comrades had all moved on, and that I would soon be left indeed alone. My situation attracted the attention of Major Savage—who was riding in rear of column—who hailed me from the trail below with, "you had better wake up from that dream up there, or you may lose your hair." I hurriedly joined the major on the descent, and as other views presented themselves, I said with some enthusiasm, "If my hair is now required, I can depart in peace, for I have here seen the power and glory of a Supreme being; the majesty of His handy-work is in that 'Testimony of the Rocks.' That mute appeal—pointing to El Capitan—illustrates it, with more convincing eloquence than can the most powerful arguments of surpliced priests." "Hold up, Doc! you are soaring too high for me; and perhaps for yourself. This is rough riding; we had better mind this devilish trail, or we shall go *soaring* over some of these slippery rocks." We, however, made the descent in safety.

Later that evening, as the company sat around the fire talking about the day's events, Bunnell suggested that they exercise one of the time honored prerogatives of discoverers and name the valley:

I suggested that this valley should have an appropriate name by which to designate it, and in a tone of pleasantry, said to Tunnehill, who was drying his wet clothing by our fire, "You are the first white man that ever received any form of baptism in this valley, and you should be considered the proper person to give a baptismal name to the valley itself." [Tunnehill had fallen in the Merced trying to cross it on horseback in high water.] He replied, "If whisky can be provided for such a ceremony, I shall be happy to participate; but if it is to be another cold-water affair, I have no desire to take a hand. I have done enough in that line for tonight." Timely jokes and ready repartee for a time changed the subject, but in the lull of this exciting pastime, some one remarked, "I like Bunnell's suggestion of giving this valley a name, and tonight is a good time to do it." "All right—if you have got one, show your hand," was the response of another. Different names were proposed, but none were satisfactory to a majority of our circle. Some romantic and foreign names were offered, but I observed that a very large number were canonical and Scripture names. From this I inferred that I was not the only one in whom religious emotions or thoughts had been aroused by the mysterious power of the surrounding scenery.

As I did not take a fancy to any of the names proposed, I remarked that "an American name would be the most appropriate;" that "I could not see any necessity for going to a foreign country for a name for American scenery—the grandest that had ever yet been looked upon. That it would be better to give it an Indian name than to import a strange and inexpressive one; that the name of the tribe who had occupied it would be more appropriate than any I had heard suggested." I then proposed "that we give the valley the name of Yo-sem-i-ty, as it was suggestive, euphonious, and certainly *American*; that by so doing, the name of the tribe of Indians which we met leaving their homes in this valley, perhaps never to return, would be perpetuated." I was here interrupted by Mr. Tunnehill, who impatiently exclaimed: "Devil take the Indians and their names! Why should we honor these vagabond murderers by perpetuating their name?" Another said: "I agree with Tunnehill; —— the Indians and their names. Mad Anthony's plan for me! Let's call this Paradise Valley." In reply, I said to the last speaker, "Still, for a young man with such *religious tendencies* they would be good objects on which to develop your Christianity." Unexpectedly, a hearty laugh was raised, which broke up further discussion, and before opportunity was given for any others to object to the name, John O'Neil, a rollicking Texan of Capt. Boling's company, vociferously announced to the whole camp the subject of our discussion, by saying, "Hear ye! Hear ye! Hear ye! A vote will now be taken to decide what name shall be given to this valley." The question of giving it the name of Yo-sem-i-ty was then explained; and upon a *viva voce* vote being taken, it was almost unanimously adopted. The name that was there and thus adopted by us, while seated around our camp fires, on the first visit of a white man to this remarkable locality, is the name by which it is now known to the world. [*Lafayette Houghton Bunnell*, DISCOVERY OF THE YOSEMITE (*1880*) *53-62*.]

## Hutchings Expedition of 1855

Four years after the Mariposa Battalion entered Yosemite, James Mason Hutchings led the first tourist party into the valley. He was living in San Francisco at the time and planned to begin publication of a California magazine in the fall of 1855. He wanted in the first issue to describe the marvelous canyon reported to exist in the central Sierra. He hired the artist Thomas Ayres to make drawings of it, gathered together some hardy companions, and followed the Battalion's footsteps through Mariposa and Wawona to the valley rim at Old Inspiration Point:

> The inapprehensible, the uninterpretable profound, was at last opened up before us. That first vision into its wonderful depths was to me the birth of an indescribable "first love" for scenic grandeur that has continued, unchangeably, to this hour, and I gratefully treasure the priceless gift.
>
> This mere glimpse of the enchanting prospect seemed to fill our soul to overflowing with gratified delight, that was only manifest in unbidden tears. Our lips were speechless from thanks-giving awe. Neither the language of tongue nor pen, nor the most perfect successes of art, can approximately present that picture. It was sublimity materialized in granite, and beauty crystallized into object forms, and both drawing us nearer to the Infinite One.
>
> It would be difficult to tell how long we looked lingeringly at this unexpected revelation; for,
> *"With thee conversing, I forget all time."*
>
> Our sketches finished—the first probably ever taken [by Thomas Ayres]—the fast-lengthening shadows admonished a postponement of that intensely pleasurable experience, and in response we hastened our descent to the camp-ground on the floor of the valley. [*James Mason Hutchings*, IN THE HEART OF THE SIERRAS *(1886) 87.*]

## Hutchings Expedition of 1859

In 1859 Hutchings returned to Yosemite in order to secure additional copy for his magazine. This time his party, which included the photographer Charles Leander Weed, used the newly blazed trail from the mining town of Big Oak Flat and first looked into the valley from high on the north rim just west of El Capitan:

> It is difficult to say whether the exciting pleasures of anticipation had quickened our pulses to the more vigorous use of our spurs, or that the horses had already smelled, in imagination at least, the luxuriant patches of grass in the great valley, or that the road was better than it had been before, certain it is, from whatever cause, we traveled faster and easier than at any previous time, and came in sight of the haze-draped summits of the mountain-walls that girdle the Yo-Semite Valley, in a couple of hours after leaving Crane Flat—distance nine miles.

Now, it may so happen that the reader entertains the idea that if he could just look upon a wonderful or an impressive scene, he could fully and accurately describe it. If so, we gratefully tender to him the use of our chair; for, we candidly confess, that we can not. The truth is, the first view of this convulsion-rent valley, with its perpendicular mountain cliffs, deep gorges, and awful chasms, spread out before us like a mysterious scroll, took away the power of thinking, much less of clothing thoughts with suitable language.

> *And I beheld when he had opened the sixth seal, and, lo, there was a great earthquake; and the sun became black as sackcloth of hair, and the moon became as blood, and the stars of heaven fell unto the earth, even as a fig tree casteth her untimely figs; when she is shaken of a mighty wind.*
>
> *And the heaven departed as a scroll when it is rolled together; and every mountain and island were moved out of their places.*
>
> *And the kings of the earth, and the great men, and the rich men, and the chief captains, and mighty men, and every bondman, and every freeman, hid themselves in the dens and in the rocks of the mountains; and said to the mountains and rocks, Fall on us, and hide us from the face of him that sitteth on the throne, and from the wrath of the Lamb: for the great day of his wrath is come; and who shall be able to stand?*

These words from Holy Writ will the better convey the impression, not of the thought, so much, but of the profound feeling inspired by that scene.

"This verily is the stand-point of silence," at length escaped in whispering huskiness from the lips of one of our number, Mr. Ewer. Let us name this spot "The Stand-point of Silence." And so let it be written in the note-book of every tourist, as it will be in his inmost soul when he looks at the appalling grandeur of the Yo-Semite valley from this spot.

When the inexpressible "first impression" had been overcome and human tongues had regained the power of speech, such exclamations as the following were uttered—"Oh! now let me die, for I am happy." "Did mortal eyes ever behold such a scene in any other land?" "The half had not been told us." "My heart is full to overflowing with emotion at the sight of so much appalling grandeur in the glorious works of God!" "I am satisfied." "This sight is worth ten years of labor," etc. etc.

A young man, named Wadlove [Waddilove], who had fallen sick with fever at Coulterville, and who, consequently, had to remain behind his party, became a member of ours; and on the morning of the second day out, experiencing a relapse, he requested us to leave him behind; but, as we expressed our determination to do nothing of the kind, at great inconvenience to himself, he continued to ride slowly along. When at Hazel Green, he quietly murmured, "I would not have started on this trip, and suffer as much as I have done this day, for ten thousand dollars." But when he arrived at this point, and looked upon the glorious wonders presented to his view, he exclaimed,

"I am a hundred times repaid now for all I have this day suffered, and I would gladly undergo a thousand times as much could I endure it, and be able to look upon another such a scene." [*James Mason Hutchings, "The Great Yo-Semite Valley" (1859-60) 158-159.*]


## *Ludlow and Bierstadt in Yosemite, 1863*

In 1863 the eastern writer and intellectual Fitz Hugh Ludlow accompanied the painter Albert Bierstadt on a cross-continent trek that ended in Yosemite. They, like the Mariposa Battalion in 1851 and Hutchings in 1855, arrived at the south rim via the Indian trail from Wawona. Ludlow thought the scene unfolding before him from Old Inspiration Point did not belong to the earth he was accustomed to seeing. So huge was it that devices used to measure other places were useless. Maybe he had found a place that God had just finished creating:

> Our dense leafy surrounding hid from us the fact of our approach to the Valley's tremendous battlement, till our trail turned at a sharp angle and we stood on "Inspiration Point." That name had appeared pedantic, but we found it only the spontaneous expression of our own feelings on the spot. We did not so much seem to be seeing from that crag of vision a new scene on the old familiar globe as a new heaven and a new earth into which the creative spirit had just been breathed. I hesitate now, as I did then, at the attempt to give my vision utterance. Never were words so beggared for an abridged translation of any Scripture of Nature.
>
> We stood on the verge of a precipice more than three thousand feet in height,—a sheer granite wall, whose terrible perpendicular distance baffled all visual computation. Its foot was hidden among haze green *spiculae*,—they might be tender spears of grass catching the slant sun on upheld aprons of cobweb, or giant pines whose tops that sun first gilt before he made gold of all the Valley.
>
> There faced us another wall like our own. How far off it might be we could only guess. When Nature's lightning hits a man fair and square, it splits his yardstick. On recovering from the stroke, mathematicians have ascertained the width of the Valley to vary between half a mile and five miles. Where we stood the width is about two.
>
> Let us leave the walls of the Valley to speak of the Valley itself, as seen from this great altitude. There lies a sweep of emerald grass turned to chrysoprase by the slant-beamed sun,—chrysoprase beautiful enough to have been the tenth foundation-stone of John's apocalyptic heaven. Broad and fair just beneath us, it narrows to a little strait of green between the butments that uplift the giant domes. Far to the westward, widening more and more, it opens into the bosom of great mountain-ranges,—into a field of perfect light, misty by its own excess,—into an unspeakable suffusion of glory created from the phoenix-pile of the dying sun. Here it lies almost as treeless as some rich old clover-mead; yonder, its luxuriant smooth grasses give way to a dense wood of cedars, oaks, and pines.

Not a living creature, either man or beast, breaks the visible silence of this inmost paradise; but for ourselves, standing at the precipice, petrified, as it were, rock on rock, the great world might well be running back in stone-and-grassy dreams to the hour when God had given him as yet but two daughters, the crag and the clover. We were breaking into the sacred closet of Nature's self-examination. What if, on considering herself, she should of a sudden, and us-ward unawares, determine to begin the throes of a new cycle,—spout up remorseful lavas from her long-hardened conscience, and hurl us all skyward in a hot concrete with her unbosomed sins? Earth below was as motionless as the ancient heavens above, save for the shining serpent of the Merced, which silently to our ears threaded the middle of the grass, and twinkled his burnished back in the sunset wherever for a space he glided out of the shadow of woods. [*Fitz Hugh Ludlow, "Seven Weeks in the Great Yo-Semite" (1864) 740, 746, 748-749.*]

### Muir's First Summer in the Sierra, 1869

John Muir arrived in San Francisco in 1868 and saw Yosemite for the first time that year. Anxious to return there, he accepted the offer of San Joaquin rancher Pat Delaney to help tend his sheep on their annual summer migration from the Central Valley to the High Sierra. Since Muir was not the principal shepherd, he had plenty of time to wander about in the Yosemite high country studying its plants and animals and searching out grand vistas. Later he revised his journal and published it as *My First Summer in the Sierra*. In the excerpt which follows he is perched on top of North Dome:

Sketching on the North Dome. It commands views of nearly all the valley besides a few of the high mountains. I would fain draw everything in sight—rock, tree, and leaf. But little can I do beyond mere outlines,—marks with meanings like words, readable only to myself,—yet I sharpen my pencils and work on as if others might possibly be benefited. Whether these picture-sheets are to vanish like fallen leaves or go to friends like letters, matters not much; for little can they tell to those who have not themselves seen similar wildness, and like a language have learned it. No pain here, no dull empty hours, no fear of the past, no fear of the future. These blessed mountains are so compactly filled with God's beauty, no petty personal hope or experience has room to be. Drinking this champagne water is pure pleasure, so is breathing the living air, and every movement of limbs is pleasure, while the whole body seems to feel beauty when exposed to it as it feels the campfire or sunshine, entering not by the eyes alone, but equally through all one's flesh like radiant heat, making a passionate ecstatic pleasure-glow not explainable. One's body then seems homogeneous through-out, sound as a crystal.

Perched like a fly on this Yosemite dome, I gaze and sketch and bask, oftentimes settling down into dumb admiration without definite hope of ever learning much, yet with the longing, unresting effort that lies at the door of hope, humbly prostrate before the vast display of God's power, and eager to offer self-denial and renunciation with eternal toil to learn any lesson in the divine manuscript.

It is easier to feel than to realize, or in any way explain, Yosemite grandeur. The magnitudes of the rocks and trees and streams are so delicately harmonized they are mostly hidden. Sheer precipices three thousand feet high are fringed with tall trees growing close like grass on the brow of a lowland hill, and extending along the feet of these precipices a ribbon of meadow a mile wide and seven or eight long, that seems like a strip a farmer might mow in less than a day. Waterfalls, five hundred to one or two thousand feet high, are so subordinated to the mighty cliffs over which they pour that they seem like wisps of smoke, gentle as floating clouds, though their voices fill the valley and make the rocks tremble. The mountains, too, along the eastern sky, and domes in front of them, and the succession of smooth rounded waves between, swelling higher, higher, with dark woods in their hollows, serene in massive exuberant bulk and beauty, tend yet more to hide the grandeur of the Yosemite temple and make it appear as a subdued subordinate feature of the vast harmonious landscape. Thus every attempt to appreciate any one feature is beaten down by the overwhelming influence of all the others. And, as if this were not enough, lo! in the sky arises another mountain range with topography as rugged and substantial-looking as the one beneath it—snowy peaks and domes and shadowy Yosemite valleys—another version of the snowy Sierra, a new creation heralded by a thunder-storm. [*John Muir*, MY FIRST SUMMER IN THE SIERRA *(1911) 174-177.*]

## *A Religious Understanding*

DURING THE NINETEENTH and early twentieth centuries writers drew their most satisfying metaphors for describing Yosemite out of the deep well of their own religious experience, as is abundantly illustrated by the previous narratives. This experience was, of course, predominantly Christian, and the Bible was not only a cistern of images that never ran dry but a story whose plot was borrowed for the Yosemite tale. In the beginning God made Yosemite:

We tarry for a little at Artist's Point, and watch for a few moments the Great Creator fashioning his Garden for man. It was just thirty-two thousand years ago by actual count, that is scientists tell us so, that God put beneath the granite crust of earth this temblor lever and raised up these temple walls. Then with a sledge of his own right arm he struck and the blow that cleft the rocks made the floor; and then he knocked out the props from beneath that floor and while it was sinking, he brought out his kit of glacier tools and rounded the domes, and scraped the walls, and carved out a way for

ALBERT BIERSTADT
[*Yosemite at Night*], 1864
Oil on canvas
Yosemite Collection

CURRIER AND IVES
*Yo-semite Falls, California*, no date
Chromolithograph
Yosemite Collection

cascade and fall and stream. And then he put his tools away and brought out and planted the seeds and made it ready and beautiful for man. [YOSEMITE OVER INDIAN TRAILS *(1909)*.]

Many writers compared the valley to the Garden of Eden; some even suggested that Yosemite was the very place itself:

Through the windings of the valley flows a river, cold as ice and clear as crystal, its source apparently being from the clouds above. There is luxuriant vegetation, and the extreme of barrenness, the softest carpet-moss and grassy lawns, and great ferns and wild roses, alternating with huge scattered rocks, where not even the lichen will cling. The traveller will note how the sunbeams brighten the summits of the giant mountains; how the sunshine creeps down the sides of the cold walls, filling the valley with flowers of golden glory, made brighter by the contrast of patches of deep shade. The valley is one vast flower-garden; plants, shrubs, and flowers of every hue cover the ground like a carpet; the eye is dazzled by the brilliancy of the color, and the air is heavy with the fragrance of a million blossoms. There are trees of five and six hundred years' growth, of immense height, and yet in comparison with the vast perpendicular clefts of rock they look like daisies beside a sycamore of the forest. One interesting writer on the subject of the Yosemite advances the theory that it is possible that the spot may have been the Eden of Scripture. [*William Seward Webb*, CALIFORNIA AND ALASKA *(1890) 66-67.*]

Perhaps the writer Webb refers to is William Simpson:

Although it is wild and grand in the highest degree, it is yet a perfect bower of beauty. Eden itself could not have been more lovely. Having now seen the Yosemite, I renounce for ever as absurd the traditions that Aden or Ceylon could have been the Garden of Paradise. Under the article "Eden," the writer in Smith's Dictionary of the Bible remarks:—"The three continents of the Old World have been subjected to the most rigorous search; from China to the Canary Isles, from the Mountains of the Moon to the coasts of the Baltic, no locality which in the slightest degree corresponded to the description of the first abode of the human race has been left unexamined. The great rivers of Europe, Asia, and Africa, have in turn done service as the Pison and Gihon of Scripture, and there remains nothing but the New World wherein the next adventurous theorist may bewilder himself in the mazes of this most difficult question." Here I register my copyright to the newest theory. The spot is not to be found in the Old World, and, in the only place left where search can be made, it has been discovered. Should any one ask me for proof, I say, "No; go and see the Yosemite for yourself, and you will seek for no more proofs!" [*William Simpson*, MEETING THE SUN: A JOURNEY ALL ROUND THE WORLD *(1874) 385-386.*]

As it was in the beginning, so it will be in the end. That the Christian heaven is urban and Yosemite wild did not deter people from thinking they were entering the New Jerusalem. William Doxey quotes the response of one tourist party to a vision of the sunset from Inspiration Point: "We spring to our feet and wave our hands, while we sing 'Hallelujah!' as the doors of this heavenly city are thrown open to receive us." (*Doxey's Guide to San Francisco and the Pleasure Resorts of California* [1897] 196.) Cora Morse had a similar experience. She looked down into the valley from Glacier Point after an evening thunderstorm:

> The Great Artist prepares his exhibit at the lower edge of "Vernal Falls," where the rainbow spreads over the ground for more than a mile following the misty spray. All colors play like lightning for about fifteen minutes, then the orange shades are lost, leaving the green and violet and blue. These, one by one, disappear while the blue alone lights the whole volume of water and reaches to "Nevada Falls" above, where the blue shades are plainly visible across its transparent body. Soon the violet, green, and orange tints are added. This stands like a band, or belt of seven hued lights against the falls.
>
> We cannot refrain from singing praises. Are we not catching a glimpse of the "Celestial City" with its "gates of pearls" and diamonds, rubies and precious stones, and its "streets of gold?" Isn't that the "Throne" over yonder, where the Day God is just laying down his silver mantle for the night? Aren't those the white robes of the blest fluttering yonder? and isn't that the "harp of a thousand strings" in time and tune to the music of the spheres? Yes, it is all there. [*Cora A. Morse*, YOSEMITE AS I SAW IT *(1896) 18-19.*]

Christians actually find themselves, of course, not in the beginning or at the end, but in the middle, in the dispensation of the church. So writers saw Yosemite as God's church, personally built by him, where all can worship until they enter the Heavenly Jerusalem:

> We fancied ourselves in a mighty cathedral, the floor of which was carpeted with velvety, variegated verdure, more beautiful than the choicest figures that can be inlaid in the rarest and costliest mosaics.
>
> It was not difficult to mark the nave, the central part of the valley, the transept,—a line of trees near the upper end which, stretching out, separated the chancel from the nave,—nor to descry, here and there, chapels and cloisters,—crevices in the rocks,—besides stalls for the retirement of the clergy, aisles leading in different directions appearing on every hand, rose windows, and a thousand fantastic mural decorations, arches supported by columns representing Gothic, Egyptian, Doric, and every other style of architecture, all canopied by the "brave o'erhanging firmament," a "majestical roof fretted with golden fire." And, rising above all, turrets and domes and spires and towers and minarets, all combining to create a vast temple as compared with which Saint Peter's at Rome, the Mosque of Saint Sophia at Constantinople, and Saint Paul's at London, sink into insignificance. [*Clark Ezra Carr*, MY DAY AND GENERATION *(1908) 102-103.*]

In his Yosemite cathedral God is especially manifest, so much so that the valley is a special chapter in his "Scripture of Nature," as Ludlow put it, where all about is "written the majesty of God." (William Baer, "A Trip to the Yosemite Falls" [1856].) Yosemite is a grand parable written in hieroglyphics:

> The towering domes, the rocky sentinels, and the rushing waterfalls in the Yosemite Valley, speak in deep thundering tones, as the Voice spoke to Moses: "The place whereon thou standest is holy ground." Everywhere in it the footprints of God's presence and tokens of God's power are discernible. This fair earth is recognized to be a mighty parable. Its manifold forms and hues are the outer folds, the waving skirts and fringes, of that garment of light in which the Invisible has robed His mysterious loveliness. There is not a leaf, nor a flower, nor a dew drop, but bears this image, and reveals to us far deeper things of God than do final causes, or evidences of design. The whole face of nature, to him who can read it aright, is covered with celestial types and hieroglyphics, marked like the dial-plate of a watch, with significant intimations of the objects and processes of the world unseen. [*John J. Powell*, WONDERS OF THE SIERRA NEVADA *(1881) 83-84.*]

Consequently, while in the valley, one need not go into a church made with human hands to hear a sermon spoken by human mouth:

> It seemed indeed, that I was making a pilgrimage to some vast cathedral shrine of Nature. The stately trees were as columns through which one finds their way along the vast colonnade, when approaching St. Peters. There is a hush in the air—you feel you are in a mighty presence. This wondrous valley —Nature's own great cathedral, where her votaries come from all lands to wonder and admire— whose cathedral spires point to heaven, whose domes have withstood the storms and tempests of all the ages, seem set apart from all the world to show forth the mighty works of Omnipotent Power. There is no church service but we listen all day to the voice of the waterfall, and at times go out to admire and worship, and be lifted up by this grand universal prayer, whose accompaniment is Nature's own choir—whose minstrelsy combines the falling of cataracts, the sighing of the breeze, the thunder of falling rocks, and whose echoes reverberate along the aisle of the cathedral, proclaiming the omnipotent power of its great architect. [*Josiah Letchworth, letter (1880).*]

In Yosemite, Faith is the eye to see by:

> It was not the purpose of the visitor to examine the Yosemite Valley with the geologist's hammer or the theodolite of the engineer. He left that laborious task to the more capable Professor Whitney, who had just arrived with all his scientific appliances, for the purpose of completing the second volume of his valuable reports. He preferred to see things with the natural eye of Faith, rather than to measure them by the calculus of Science; for in that grandest of God's earthly temples, inquiry were profanation. We had not the fortitude to ask "why is it so?" under the shadow of mightier than the

Pyramids, and amid the prophetic eloquence of loud talking cataracts that leap down from the heights, foaming and soaring, a thousand feet at a bound. But resting on the bank of the sweet and beautiful Merced, he said to himself: "I lie down on my face in this Valley of Miracles: I put off my shoes at the feet of these watery Sinais, dismayed and humbled by the awful proclamations of Nature's sublimest prophets, crying perpetually: 'The cedars of the mountain stretch their arms to God; the cataract sends up its everlasting anthem in his praise; the ocean throbs at his touch; the procession of the stars moves at his command, and even the trefoil lifts its three-fold palm from the Valley, a reverent little worshipper in the grand temple of the Universe.'" [*"Merced—The Alf of YoSemite" (1867)*.]

In this natural cathedral skeptics are converted:

To attempt to describe the grandeur of this scene [from Inspiration Point] would be folly; to tell of the feelings of awe, of humility, or reverence, which are here aroused, is all that can be done. He who tries to believe there is no God is here at once converted in the twinkling of an eye; and his feelings of reverence and veneration, blended with love and beauty, force him to a worship at once pure and creedless. [*John Erastus Lester*, THE ATLANTIC TO THE PACIFIC *(1873) 177*.]

My first view of the Yosemite Valley, as I came out of the Wawona tunnel, was an overwhelming illumination; my spirit soared and my life assumed new meaning. [*Milton Goldstein*, THE MAGNIFICENT WEST: YOSEMITE *(1973) 4*.]

In all of the passages in this section Yosemite is a holy sign. Its grandeur is evidence for the existence of God, its peaks point to God, its waterfalls speak his name. God sits invisibly on its mountains the way he sat invisibly on his ancient throne, the ark of Israel:

But to appreciate the wonders of Yosemite, one must go into the solemn depths of this chasm where the wild Merced thunders its deep anthem to the glory of the Eternal; or to the awesome heights where the majesty of the Infinite sits enthroned on rock and snow. [*Lehmer*, YOSEMITE NATIONAL PARK *(1912)*.]

Moreover, just as once Isaiah actually saw God seated upon his ark throne (see Isaiah 6), latter-day prophets can see him in Yosemite. The eye of faith can be shut and the eye of knowledge opened:

So we went on, rather flagging as the day advanced, till we came to Inspiration Point, where we were to have our first view of the remarkable place we had come so far to see. As we neared the spot, silence fell upon the party—all were busy with their own thoughts. Faith was soon to be turned into sight. With our own eyes we should soon verify what had been told us of this wonderful valley, like

Louis Prang
*Yosemite Valley*, ca. 1869
Chromolithograph after a painting by Thomas Hill
Courtesy, Boston Public Library

G. F. ARMSTRONG
*Yosemite Valley*, no date
Oil on canvas
Yosemite Collection

which there was said to be no other. That supreme moment, desired so long, hoped for through years, was near at hand. Then there was, after all, a vague uncertainty as to what the sight would be to us individually. Would our hopes or our fears be realized? The veil would soon be lifted, and we should know for ourselves—no longer see through the eyes of others. We dismounted at a little distance, and were soon on the edge of the precipice. There it was—this trough hewn out of the mountains. Awe-struck I stood, mute, and almost immovable. I should have been glad to be all alone in this first interview with God manifest. Whatever of majesty that is made up of imaginable strength and massiveness was there. Whatever of sublimity, inconceivable height and unsounded depth can give was there. [*Mary Cone*, TWO YEARS IN CALIFORNIA *(1876) 211-212.*]

The overpowering sense of the sublime, of awful desolation, of transcending marvelousness and unexpectedness that swept over us, as we reined our horses sharply out of green forests and stood upon high jutting rock that overlooked this upheaving sea of granite mountains, beholding far down its rough lap this vale of beauty of meadow and grove and river—such tide of feeling, such stoppage of ordinary emotions, comes at rare intervals in any life. It was the confrontal of God face to face, as in great danger, in solemn, sudden death. [*Samuel Bowles*, ACROSS THE CONTINENT *(1866) 223.*]

When a lady who had climbed Inspiration Point was asked what she saw, answered: "I see God." [*Rev. Dr. Hunt, sermon (1871).*]

In sum, it is clear that many people saw in Yosemite the embodiment, not to say the incarnation, of the Judeao-Christian god. Its outstanding attributes, power and glory, were likewise his. Charles Carleton Coffin said that he was "overwhelmed by the scene" at Inspiration Point and "gazed as one who has suddenly passed into a higher existence." Standing in the midst of "the transcendant glory of the New Jerusalem," he witnessed "beauty, grandeur, majesty, immensity, and omnipotence." He is describing Yosemite but he could just as well be describing God. No wonder he reported hearing in the many-voiced waters of the Merced "the song of the redeemed swelling upward through the evening air," a "*Te Deum laudamus* ever ascending." (Charles Carleton Coffin, *Our New Way Round the World* [1869] 483-484.)

## *Fear and Trembling*

THE ONLY DISCORD in the Hallelujah Choruses we have heard thus far is Hutchings' quotation from the book of Revelation. While gazing on Yosemite glory, he remembered, of all things, a passage describing the wrath of God and the fear of men:

*And I beheld when he had opened the sixth seal, and, lo, there was a great earthquake; and the sun became black as sackcloth of hair, and the moon became as blood, and the stars of heaven fell unto the earth, even as a fig tree casteth her untimely figs; when she is shaken of a mighty wind.*

*And the heaven departed as a scroll when it is rolled together; and every mountain and island were moved out of their places.*

*And the kings of the earth, and the great men, and the rich men, and the chief captains, and mighty men, and every bondman, and every freeman, hid themselves in the dens and in the rocks of the mountain; and said to the mountains and rocks, Fall on us, and hide us from the face of him that sitteth on the throne, and from the wrath of the Lamb: for the great day of his wrath is come; and who shall be able to stand?*

Interestingly enough, Hutchings was not the only early Yosemite writer to think of God's wrath while surveying Yosemite from Inspiration Point. A correspondent of the *Hartford Courant*, whose last name was Gollek, sent to his paper the following account that the *Mariposa Gazette* reprinted:

After proceeding about a mile we dismounted, and leaving our horses were led a short distance off the trail to a high and wild projection, known as "Inspiration Point," where an almost entire view of the valley burst upon us, as it were instantaneously. To describe my emotions and feelings at that time would be impossible; all I could do was to sit down and look in silence with breath subdued. Down, far down below us, lay the valley in all its beauty, with the Merced river sinuously winding its course, and on either side, towering to the heavens, shutting it in from the outer world, stood the high, vertical haze-draped walls of granite rocks. The sight in all its vastness was bewildering to the senses. For a time it all appeared to be a dream of indescribable grandeur, and of infinite immensity, if I may thus express myself. As soon as the mind recovers from its first shock, it turns upward to Him who created all this, and passages from Holy-Writ are at once impressed on the mind. "Therefore, I will shake the heavens, and the earth shall remove out of her place, in the wrath of the Lord of Hosts, and in the day of his fierce anger." [*"Yo Semite Valley" (1867).*]

After hearing that the beauty of the valley and its "haze-draped walls" amounts to "a dream of indescribable grandeur," one expects to read about God's glory rather than his "fierce anger." The following passage by the painter Charles Dorman Robinson belongs in this same context, for it too juxtaposes the beautiful and the terrible, security and great danger. Robinson is writing to publicize the Wawona Hotel and the new road from Wawona to Glacier Point:

We can only bid the indulgent reader good-bye, with this parting advice: That if he is bound to Yosemite, either go into, or come out of, that wonderful valley by way of the new Glacier Point road, if he would see summits upon summits of snow, and miles upon miles of the most beautiful trees living, and ride in security over that great table land where the blasts of winter wreathe columns and sprays of snow high in the air; where the stately firs roar an echoing sympathy to the far distant yell and scream, roar and crash of the cyclone of Pacific's fury, and where the fury of foam and spray of ocean is answered by equal fury of blasted pine, writhing and far reaching snow banner of the high Sierra, and the banner of snow of the mountain, and the banner of foam of the sea wave, sing eternal glory to Him, and defiance and death to man, until such time as the voice is heard and the fiat goes forth, "Peace, be still." [*Charles Dorman Robinson*, THE WAWONA HOTEL.]

These curious passages afford an opportunity to probe deeper into the fullness of the Yosemite experience. Perhaps because Yosemite shares glory and power with God, it also shares his wrath, for the obverse of his love is his anger, and the opposite of redemption is damnation. In the following passage by H. E. Wilson, Yosemite's walls act out a divine prerogative:

It is utterally beyond the power of language to convey any impression of the awe-inspiring majesty of the walls of solid granite that enclose the Valley on every side, darkly frowning and seemingly overhanging, as though to threaten with instant annihilation any who denied their power. [*Wilson*, THE LORE AND THE LURE OF YOSEMITE *(1928) 32.*]

Members of the Mariposa Battalion, whose imaginations were influenced by the danger of their mission and apparently by exaggerated descriptions the Indians gave them, were the first to describe Yosemite as Hell. By no means were they the last:

This valley has something diabolical and wild about it which seems to overpower all detail, leaving only the most marked features visible. This is no longer the rich and enchanting country of Java, nor smiling Japan, nor Switzerland with its glaciers. It is the grandeur of naked and barren rock! One might think that the Creator, in a moment of anger, had with one great blow of a sword cut through gigantic blocks of granite. A chasm, more than a thousand yards deep, has been made in the rock; precipitous bare walls, smooth as the glacis of a fort, three thousand feet high, reflect the rays of the sun, while the bottom of the valley is in black shadow. It is one of those views that impress without charming, and almost inspire terror. [*Ludovic Marquis de Beauvoir*, PEKIN, JEDDO, AND SAN FRANCISCO *(1872) 258-259.*]

Wearied out with a day of sight-seeing I lie upon the porch at Hutchings', gaze and think. To the northwest is El Capitan, glorified in the soft moonlight; opposite Yosemite Fall, to the right the Royal Arches, over all this wondrous sky, and all around us monster battlements with shrubby fringe, till we seem to be walled in far down in the depths of the earth, shut out from human hope or help. [*J. H. Beadle*, THE UNDEVELOPED WEST; OR FIVE YEARS IN THE TERRITORIES *(1873) 278.*]

The impression one gets of this underworld from these awful heights [she is on Eagle Peak], is silence, sleep, death. Encompassing us like a great "cloud of witnesses," these eternal towering rocks are standing. Not a whisper reaches us from the yawning gulfs and bottomless chasms, which seem to possess the power to draw us downward into their destructive embrace. [*Morse*, YOSEMITE AS I SAW IT *(1896) 21.*]

Related to these almost Miltonic descriptions are images of Yosemite as a prison whose walls seem liable at any moment to topple over, making escape impossible. We have already seen that even so great a rhapsodist as Ludlow could not keep such dire thoughts out of his mind:

My first impression of the valley, with the towering granite walls that surround it, was that of a vast natural prison. [*Edmund Bickness, compiler,* RALPH'S SCRAP BOOK *(1905) 419.*]

We were now hemmed in on either side by these granite walls appearing as though if they should topple over, our escape would be impossible. [*J. S. Hutchinson, letter (1857).*]

And one writer thinks that preachers might well use the view from Glacier Point to illustrate the reality of imminent damnation:

To approach and view the scene below is simply appalling, for one is looking into the open tomb of the grandest grandeur of the Creator's handiwork, supplemented by the multiplied debris of revolving ages and the effective work of the recurring seasons, and the toiling elements for thousands of years. Here is the grandest rostrum on earth. From this commanding point the illustrative preacher might illustrate the realities of the bottomless pit to his sinful hearers, pointing them to the open abyss before them, and inviting them to "view the place where they must shortly lie." [*Richard C. Hunt, "California Letters" (1893).*]

Dark and unsettling thoughts occur to people partly because of Yosemite's naturally imposing character, especially when seen at dusk with black shadows on its floor or in the winter with thick clouds as a roof. Wilson gives a good clue for an additional and deeper reason. The passage quoted above continues:

If man ever feels his utter insignificance, his infinitesimal importance as a mere atom in the scheme of things, it should be when gazing upon this scene of appalling grandeur so charmingly blended with transcendent loveliness. [*Wilson, 32.*]

By a process that is not easily explained but psychologically is terribly real, Yosemite's immensity makes people feel tiny, insignificant, and therefore, worthless. Their comparative littleness reminds them of their shortcomings (in religious terms, their sinfulness), so that they believe they are the objects of a cosmic anger. The resulting dread is simply more than some can take:

The impression upon every thoughtful mind is deep. Sometimes it is overpowering. On the trail toward Gentry's I met two men from Illinois, on their way down. They succeeded in getting up as far as Hutchings' [opposite Yosemite Falls, about where Sentinel Bridge is today]. After remaining an hour, they turned about, and came directly back, the same afternoon. When asked why, they said, they could not explain it, only that the impression upon their minds was insupportable. They appeared to be intelligent men. [*Rev. Isaac Mast*, THE GUN, ROD AND SADDLE; OR, NINE MONTHS IN CALIFORNIA *(1875) 172.*]

But Yosemite does not let people remain in this state of anguish. Its "appalling grandeur" is "blended with transcendent loveliness," as Wilson put it. At the same time they feel cast down by their puniness they are lifted up into the sublime. This dual movement of the emotions in response to Yosemite scenery makes the human experience there intriguingly problematic and wonderfully complicated. The following three passages are sensitive accounts of this complexity, all in all three of the most interesting narratives on record:

The road has been getting gradually wilder and the hills sterner. Immense granite rocks rest on the mountain above the trail with a threatening aspect. In some places they appear to have fallen and carried large pine trees along with them. In one place I saw where a large pine tree had torn up a rock in its fall, exactly as a dentist extracts a tooth with his pincers. This afternoon, when about two miles from the entrance of the valley, we saw the Bridal Veil, the first fall in the valley. It looked like a silver thread in the distance and relieved the solemn grandeur of the surrounding hills.

As we approach the valley it grows ever wilder, and when we commence the descent we compare it involuntarily to the entrance to the infernal regions. The mountains that are in view are covered with great white rocks. The trail is over rocks, and a little stream below us tumbles and rushes over its rocky bottom as if it were mad. It is without exception the wildest scene I have ever seen. The only flowers that grow here are the beautiful scarlet ice plant, as it is called, and some fungi. The steep toilsome descent is at last accomplished. We came in view of all the party stretched on the ground beneath the shade of a tree. I am sorry to say my fortitude gave way. My foot pained me. I was very tired and threw myself exhausted on the ground.

After half an hour's rest we again proceeded on our way, and what a change! The desolation of the way we had passed was not visible to us. We rode through beautiful green meadows, under the shady branches of trees, and the fragrance of the wild honeysuckle was a pleasant exchange for the reflection of the sun's rays from the great white rocks. To the right of us was what is called a "Cathedral" in the gothic style, and where could there be a church more magnificent? We rode on, at our left "El Capitan," a man wrapped in a Spanish cloak with a slouched hat. We drew rein on the banks of the Merced, where it was very still and deep, and lay down on our blankets under the protection of the "sentinel." Never did the beauty of the Twenty-Third Psalm present itself so before me. I had been frightened and disturbed and was very weary, and the words, "He maketh me to lie down in green pastures; he leadeth me beside the *still waters.*—Yea, though I walk through the valley of the shadow of death, I will fear no evil; for thou art with me; thy rod and thy staff they comfort me," filled me with quiet and peace. We had been walking through the valley of the shadow of death, as it seemed. By my request the camp was called "Stillwater Camp." [*Sarah Haight, diary, May 20, 1858.*]

The valley here is quite narrow, and its stony and rugged surface, is densely overshadowed with trees, thoroughly obstructing a view of the valley, and suggesting the thought that after all, the place may not be equal to its representation. A half hour's ride, however, will soon dispell this despondency, as opening suddenly into a luxuriantly matted prairie, of at least a mile and a half in width, the immense parapets and walls of this the grandest and most sublime of Nature's mighty temples, burst at once upon the astonished eye. The valley is no longer a simple feature of history—subdued you feel yourself a mere atom, in its immediate and overpowering presence! Though on a plain, three quarters of a mile from the base of the wall on either side, in looking up to their dizzy summits you can seemingly realize that a hundred centuries, from a height of nearly four thousand feet are about to hurl the crumbling granite of their fury upon your helpless and insignificant head.—Catching a little of their inspiration, you look again, and behold them standing in their immaculate strength; firm, peaceful and sublime as the Diety that presides over all.

   The afternoon of the first day of our arrival, was spent in refreshment and quiet admiration—the evening with its gorgeous sunset came on, crowning each mountain peak and each hill top, with the exquisite and charming colors of a mellow and golden livery. Deepening into twilight, the great amphitheater, in which we were the diminutive and silent worshippers, assumed a ten fold solemnity.—Imagination became doubly intensified and active, requiring little effort in calling forth either the dire and fearful images of terror, or the most sublime conceptions of heavenly grandeur. Over forty miles from the nearest settlement, in a mountain wilderness and in the centre of a valley thirteen miles in length with an average of two in width; surrounded on all sides except the lower, by the impregnable granite walls, extending from twenty-eight hundred to over four thousand feet in height, and associating the distant roar of eight distinct water falls, the place at once assumed all the characteristics of terror, and the mind naturally retraced the time when "the Earth shook and trembled, and when the foundations of the world was seen;"—when, with the upheaving of internal fires, the solid rocks were rent asunder, and in the dread roar of crumbling mountains, the valley first assumed the rude form which time and the elements have since clothed with the verdure of an almost perpetual spring. [*J. W. O. "Yo-Semite" (1858).*]

Only a few miles from Peregoy's, and we were on Inspiration Point, looking down on the mighty Mecca of our pilgrimage,—on awful depth and vastness, wedded to unimagined brightness and loveliness,—a sight that appalled, while it attracted; a sublime terror; a beautiful abyss; the valley of the shadow of God!

On my first night in the valley, the strangeness of my surroundings, a sort of sombre delight that took possession of me, would not let me sleep for several hours. Once I rose and looked out, or tried to look out. The sky was clouded; it seemed to me the stars drew back from the abyss. It was filled with night and sound. I could not see the mighty rocks that walled us in, but a sense of their shadow was upon me. There was in the awe I felt no element of real dread or fear, but it was thrilled by fantastic terrors. I thought of Whitney's theory of the formation of the great pit, by subsidence. What if it should take another start in the night, and settle a mile or two with us, leaving the trail by which we descended, dangling in the air, and the cataracts all spouting away, with no outlet! But in the morning the jolly sun peered down upon us, laughing, as much as to say, "There you are, are you?" and the sweet, cool winds dipped down from the pines and the snows, the great fall shouted and danced all the way down his stupendous rocky stairway. It seems to me that darkness is darker and light lighter in the Yosemite than anywhere else on earth.

Yet, in the midst of its utmost brightness and beauty, you are more or less oppressed with a realization of some sudden convulsion of nature, that here rent the rocks asunder, that shook the massive mountain land till the bottom dropped out; or of the mighty force of drifting driving glaciers, grinding, carving, just ploughing their way down from the "High Sierra," leaving this stupendous furrow behind them. Somehow you feel that Nature has not done with this place yet. Such a grand, abandoned workshop invites her to return. The stage of this great tragic theatre of the elements waits, perhaps, for some terrible afterpiece.

I found it impossible to work here, or even to talk fluently or forcibly on what I knew about the Yosemite. The theme mastered me. I noticed that there were few singing-birds about, and was told by an old guide that they, with most animals, were afraid of the valley. Poetic thoughts and gay fancies seem struck with a like fear. You are for a time mentally unnerved; but you feel that in your powerlessness you are gaining power; in your silence, more abundant expression. [*Grace Greenwood*, NEW LIFE IN NEW LANDS *(1873) 320, 325-328.*]

## *Humbug!*

"THE *Fall* of the Yosemite, so called, is a humbug." So declared Horace Greeley on his summer visit to the valley in 1859 (*New York Tribune*, September 24, 1859). While he thought the remainder of Yosemite "the most unique and majestic of Nature's marvels," many others have thought his description apt for the valley as a whole and all its contents: domes, spires, trees, as well as waterfalls.

Naturally Yosemite lovers have risen to its defense, saying that perhaps one needs to take more time, or see it in another season, or at another time of day, or with another pair of eyes. This last suggestion expresses what the devout really feel: that the non-appreciative are Philistines. The truth, of course, is that disbelievers are as honest and as sincerely motivated as believers, and their testimony is an important part of the Yosemite story. To Derrick Dodd Yosemite looks like the stage set for a heavenly drama:

> Suddenly the stage swings out upon the brow of a mountain, the horses are stopped, and, pointing his whip forward into space, the driver ejaculates, *"Inspiration Point!"* This is the famous spot from which the first view of the Yosemite Valley is had, and the passengers crane forward and gaze with as much eagerness as if the PEARLY GATES OF THE HEREAFTER were themselves ajar. Now, with the full expectation of being instantly denounced by the guide-book writers, sat upon by the Valley Commissioners, and excommunicated by the public at large, the writer wishes to record his honest conviction that this first glimpse of the valley is a disappointing one. This arises, doubtless, from three causes—first, the disadvantage of viewing an object of great altitude—like Niagara, for instance—from a level with its top; second, on account of the extreme rarification of the air in the vicinity, and last, from the exaggerated conception of the general proportions of the valley, resultant upon the descriptions of "gush-writers."
>
> In fact, the whole landscape strikes the beholder for the moment as a pocket-edition of what he expected to see. So easily does the eye take in the whole scene, that one receives the involuntary impression that he is looking at a painting, or an unusually good "set" in a theatre. [*Derrick Dodd*, SUMMER SAUNTERINGS *(1882) 109-110.*]

Stewart Edward White's response is interesting because he uses aesthetic categories identical to John Muir's. He looks at the combination of individual elements, but, unlike Muir, he finds that they do not make a whole pleasing to the imagination:

> Yosemite is not as interesting nor as satisfying to me as some of the other big box canyons. In Yosemite everything is jumbled together, apparently for the benefit of the tourist with a linen duster and but three days' time at his disposal. He can turn from the cliff-headland to the dome, from the dome to the half dome, to the glacier formation, the granite slide and all the rest of it, with hardly the necessity of stirring his feet. Nature has put samples of all her works here within reach of his cataloguing vision. Everything is crowded in together, like a row of houses in forty-foot lots. The mere things themselves are here in profusion and wonder, but the appropriate spacing, the approach, the surrounding of subordinate detail which should lead in artistic gradation to the supreme feature —these things, which are a real and essential part of esthetic effect, are lacking utterly for want of room. The place is not natural scenery; it is a junk-shop, a storehouse, a sample-room wherein the

Washington F. Friend
[*Yosemite Falls*], 1870
Watercolor
Courtesy, Bancroft Library

James D. Smillie
*Tenaya Cañon from Glacier Point*
J. Filmer, engraver
From *Picturesque America*
Yosemite Collection

James D. Smillie
*Big Trees, Mariposa Grove*
J. Filmer, engraver
From *Picturesque America*
Yosemite Collection

CONSTANCE GORDON-CUMMING
[*Nevada Fall*], 1878
Watercolor
Yosemite Collection

elements of natural scenery are to be viewed. It is not an arrangement of effects in accordance with the usual laws of landscape, but abnormality, a freak of Nature.

It is grand beyond any possible human belief; and no one, even a nerve-frazzled tourist, can gaze on it without the strongest emotion. Only it is not so intimately satisfying as it should be. It is a show. You do not take it into your heart. "Whew!" you cry. "Isn't that a wonder!" then after a moment, "Looks just like the photographs. Up to sample. Now let's go." [*Stewart Edward White*, THE MOUNTAINS *(1920) 202-203.*]

Olive Logan's account is sarcastic and irreverent. Hers is a novel method of dealing with the inability of words to describe Yosemite:

And now begins the weary trudge again. Oh, positively we shall never live through it. We are obliged to be lifted from our horses every two or three miles, and placed under the shade of trees to rest. The sun creeps higher and higher. It pours its burning rays upon our aching heads, for we are again mounted. The pack-mule runs away; we all run with unpleasant regularity after it, our horses trotting like trip-hammers, and beating the very breath out of our bodies. And so on and on and on we go. Eight miles! It is eighty! At length we reach the precipice which is to conduct us into the Valley.

(I have requested the printer to leave a blank space here. I think it will be more eloquent than words.)

Also here, to represent the dreary period of suffering which elapsed after we began the steep descent of the precipice, and until we reached the goal of our hopes—Hutchings's Hotel.

The dawn breaks in the morning of the next day, and, shining red as fire through the pine knots of the log-cabin where Hutchings dwells, strikes our leaden eyelids and bids us arise. Reluctantly we do so. This is the end of our wanderings. Here is the great prize to obtain a view of which we have come so many weary miles. Now we are to be repaid for all. We make a hurried toilet, and as quickly as our stiffened limbs will permit, we drag out to see the view which shall awe us, shall make us lose our identity, shall cause us to feel as though we were in the spirit land.

And what do we see? Tall rocks, a few tall trees, a high and narrow waterfall, a pretty little river! No more. A lovely natural scene, I grant you; but oh! where in this broad and beautiful land of ours are not lovely natural scenes the rule? Words cannot tell the feeling of cold despair which came over me and all our party as we looked about us. Was it for this we had so suffered! O Englishman, Englishman, how painfully correct was your report! [An Englishman at the Grand Hotel in San Francisco told Logan, "You may take my word for it, it's a trip that *don't pay*."] In truth and very truth, it does not pay.

We never rallied from that first impression.

"But that stone wall is nearly a mile high."

It may be so, but does not look it; and if it did, the stars are higher, and, thank God, the stars shine at home!

"That waterfall is eleven times higher than Niagara."

Indeed! it looks like a fireman's hose playing over the top of Stewart's store.

But we try to make the best of it, once there. "Let's say it *does* pay," says the jolly Tapley of our party. "Yes, let's sit on the banks of this lovely river." We do so. A companionable but not welcome watersnake does so also, and we leave him in possession.

By another day some of us are well enough to mount again and begin our search after Beauty. We find an occasional rattlesnake, unlimited fatigue, and the tombstone of a man who was kicked to death by his horse. The trips are very wearying, the scenery very grand, very beautiful, but we are in no condition to enjoy it. We never get in such condition, and the universal verdict with us is that if every one of the waterfalls in Yo Semite were magnified, every one of its granite domes were an Olympus, if its rivers were the Rhine, and its valley the fairy gardens of Versailles, the sight of it would not repay one for the suffering involved in getting to it. And the plain truth is that nine out of ten who visit Yo Semite think this, but they will not say what they think.

O travelled monkey! Dare to tell the truth, why do you not? Because you are afraid some other travelled monkey will say you "can't appreciate" the scenery which it makes your head ache to look at, and your bones ache to get at. Because you are a coward, or because you know you have made an idiot of yourself, and flung away your money by handfuls, and endured the tortures of purgatory; and you are ashamed to confess yourself so easily taken in and done for—man of the world that you are. But I am only a woman, and I confess all. [*Olive Logan, "Does It Pay to Visit Yo Semite?"* *(1870) 505-507.*]

## A Natural Understanding

IN THE BEGINNING Yosemite was God's book written in scenic script. The early painters of huge canvases, the mammoth-plate photographers, and the writers of grandiloquent prose deciphered his sublime handwriting and copied his message in their works of art. As early as the end of the nineteenth century, however, people were reading the copy rather than the original. Yosemite became a work of art. We have just heard the testimony of Derrick Dodd and Stewart Edward White on this point. A new way of seeing Yosemite was needed.

Stephen Mather and the people associated with him in the nascent National Park Service staged a revolution in perspective during the second and third decades of the twentieth century. According to them Yosemite was a book written by nature in a language that science could best understand. They appointed a cadre of park naturalists and assigned them the dual tasks of learning nature's grammar and teaching it to the public. They did not have to start from scratch, of course. Like all revolutions, this one had its antecedents. The members of the Whitney survey, John Muir, and Joseph LeConte had already keyed out Yosemite using geological as well as religious field guides. The education movement of the early twentieth century was a revolution because the scientific method was so thoroughly adopted in studying Yosemite and because the results of scientific research were so exclusively used to explain the park to visitors. The revolutionaries were so successful that by the mid-1920s their creed had become the official position of the National Park Service. An announcement in *Yosemite Nature Notes* for June 12, 1923 reads:

### SERVING THE YOSEMITE VISITOR

The federal government serves the Yosemite visitor in many ways besides providing for his physical comfort. It is the aim of the National Park Service to help the vacationist not only to see and enjoy the wonders of the Park, but also to understand nature in its many phases.

Robert Sterling Yard and Arno B. Cammerer were two early spokesmen for this new point of view. In the selections which follow they explain clearly and eloquently the scientific agenda and the reasons for adopting it. Both borrow the terminology of the apologists for a religious interpretation of Yosemite, but now nature is the great master who has signed the canvas, or, as Cammerer puts it, "nature herself is the lecturer." Neither of them intend to suggest that God is not the ultimate cause of Yosemite. He merely recedes into the background:

The first emotion inspired by the sight of Yosemite is surprise. Hard on the heels of astonishment comes realization of the park's supreme beauty. And lastly comes the higher emotion which is born of knowledge. It is only when one reads in these inspired rocks the stirring story of their making that pleasure reaches its fulness. The added joy of the collector upon finding that the unsigned canvas, which he bought only for its beauty, is the last work of a great master, and was associated with the romance of a famous past is here duplicated. Written history never was more romantic nor more graphically told than that which Nature has inscribed upon the walls of these vast canyons, domes and monoliths in a language which man has learned to read. [*Robert Sterling Yard*, THE BOOK OF THE NATIONAL PARKS *(1919) 36-37.*]

I have just been to the Mesa Verde, the Yosemite, and to the Grand Canyon national parks, and in them have seen three of the most magnificent exhibits of the world, reserved for all time in their natural condition for enjoyment, recreation and health of our people. The tremendously mounting annual visiting list to the parks evidences the joyful enthusiastic use made of the recreational facilities of the great national wonderlands. To the observant visitor, however, soon comes the realization that aside from the recreational values, the national parks are from an education standpoint—biologic, historic, geologic and botanic—really the outdoor classrooms of the country; that, in fact, the future may see in them no less great educational centers of learning than a means to health and pleasure.

Men of science find the national parks prolific fields for investigation and observation, and the results of their studies are valuable additions to the literature on the parks as well as important contributions to science. It is not, however, alone to men of erudition or to students that the educational aspects of the parks appeal, but nature has written her lessons so boldly, so plain to the eye, that they are unconsciously imprinted on the mind of any observer. The work of water, the work of ice, the work of winds, the work of rock and mineral forming agencies, all these processes that are studies in our textbooks on geology are illustrated in the national parks on a magnificent scale and so readily discernible that nature herself is the lecturer.

Each of our national parks has a marked personality of its own and vividly illustrates some force of nature which has resulted in its making. The supreme beauty of the Yosemite Valley inevitably causes the beholder to wonder how nature made it. It does not lessen wonder to learn that it was through the slow, persistent wear of running water and glacier ice that the chasm was formed. [*Arno B. Cammerer, "The National Parks, Our Outdoor Classrooms" (1923) 47, 50.*]

Harold Bryant of California Fish and Game, Ansel Hall, Chief Park Naturalist in the early twenties, and Carl Russell, his successor, were the leading apostles of the education movement in Yosemite. Bryant began the Yosemite Nature Guide Service in 1920 as a joint venture between his department and the National Park Service. Visitors that summer could use the services of a "nature guide." An article in *Yosemite Nature Notes*, April, 1924, describes for a curious public this brave new being. The phrase "read the trail side as a book" was the motto of the reformers and appeared on many of their publications:

### YOSEMITE'S TRAIL SCHOOL

On the first day of June, 1924, the Yosemite Nature Guide Service will begin its fifth year. Since the beginning of the service in 1920 by Dr. H. C. Bryant, an ever-growing number of park visitors have learned to know and enjoy the opportunities it offers, yet there are many prospective Yosemite visitors who will wonder what a nature guide service may be.

A nature guide is a very human sort of an individual who can "read the trail side as a book." In the Yosemite they are chosen scientists who are not only intimately acquainted with the Sierra wild life but who are enthusiastic in aiding others to know it as well. The annual exodus of the American public to the out-of-doors has created a genuine demand for such a service. The national parks have, of course, become great centers for the hundreds of thousands who migrate to summer play grounds,

T. F. LAYCOCK
[*Yosemite Falls*], no date
Oil on canvas
Yosemite Collection

and it is natural that the Government should provide the educational service that aids in spreading the message of the parks.

Experience has shown that the average Yosemite visitor is in a receptive mood—more than that he feels a lack of knowledge of the abundance of wild life about him. As a camper he finds himself a part of the community of nature and strikes up a friendship with the wild-life members of the community, and thus it becomes possible for the nature guide service to link education with recreation.

This season thousands of Yosemite visitors will go afield with nature guides. They will be escorted to moss covered stream sides where they may observe that most interesting of birds, the water ouzel, feed its young; they will learn first hand of the great variety of bird songs and the bird musicians; the magnificent trees of the Sierra will be made familiar; a wealth of wild flowers, rare and common alike, may be classed as intimate acquaintances by many; every plant and animal of the trail side will occasion a story—the very cliffs will disclose a romance to those who read. [YOSEMITE NATURE NOTES, April, 1924.]

Bryant himself, in the training manual for ranger naturalists, is more fervent. He takes an educator's point of view, but uses the rhetoric of a preacher:

A nature guide must make eyes to see, and ears to hear, in fact stimulate all the senses. A nature guide strives to make amateur naturalists of his students. But most important of all, the method used must be such as to inspire students to continue to seek out nature's secrets wherever they find themselves.

Visitors to our recreation areas are hungry for useful information regarding natural phenomena. Everyone who seeks the Sierra for a vacation does so either from curiosity or from a sense of appreciation, and among them all there is hardly a person who does not respond with some show of emotion when a deer bounds across the road, or a fish jumps in a stream. The responsive time is the time to approach them, to point out to many of them their unrealized, undeveloped fund for the enjoyment of Nature, and in others to satisfy an already awakened craving for information. [*Harold C. Bryant*, YOSEMITE RANGER-NATURALIST MANUAL *(1929) 28-29.*]

1920 was also the year that Ansel Hall gave definite shape to the idea of a Yosemite museum. Publication of the *Yosemite Nature Notes* as a joint venture of the Yosemite Museum Association (later the Yosemite Natural History Association), the Museum, and the Nature Guide Service began in 1922. By means of wildlife displays in the Museum and brief articles on Yosemite flora and fauna in *Nature Notes*, Hall and his compatriots hoped to further their "missionary" work of providing visitors with a "complete understanding" of the park. Herbert Maier implicitly compares museums in national parks with the Church Militant:

The educational value of the park museums is thus not to be measured by the specimens in their cases. They are to the nature study movement what recharging stations are to a transcontinental telephone line; nay, more; they are militant propagation centers; and that movement is probably the least dubious and the most promising among the "movements" of our day and country, with its manifold implications of benefit to knowledge, citizenship and the good life, to conservation. If it is next considered that these museums draw their public from all over the country (and from beyond it) their radius of influence is seen to be impressive. And if one happens to be an enthusiast in the cause he will end by feeling that the national park museums are a contribution—a very modest one, but a contribution—toward making a better America for Americans, and—better Americans for America. [*Herbert Maier*, YOSEMITE NATURE NOTES 5 (1926) 37.]

To spread the message of the national parks over the entire country and to provide teachers for the educational movement, the Yosemite School of Field Natural History opened in 1925 under the leadership of the indefatigable Harold Bryant. It offered college level courses in all aspects of "reading the trail side." Ruth Moore tells what she learned in school during the summer of 1934:

We grew "trail conscious" going into the High Country with Joe Dixon. We discovered that there is more to hiking than just putting one foot ahead of the other. We grew alert to more than just the pair of pants ahead of us on the trail, and learned to read the trail over which we traveled, and the far trail ahead as well.

Many times we found the loping trail of the mountain coyote along a stream bed, the track showing his claws and a heel pad about one-half the width of the track. There was one early morning in Kerrick Meadows that we could read the story of a chase in a nearby dry stream bed. The trail of a swiftly running coyote followed that of a bounding deer in flight.

The most graceful of all the tracks we met was that of the mule deer, with its continual curve pointing forward to the center. Some of us learned to tell the sex of the deer by their footprints. The female has the sharper hoofs and the narrower foot, while the male has more rounded points to the hoofs.

It was on our trail from Glen Aulin to Lake Tenaya that some of us saw a rather curious Sierra marmot, or woodchuck—better called "rockchuck"—with its red bushy tail and yellow cheeks. Mr. Dixon had previously pointed out the marmot's tracks to us, and we recognized them in the dust of the trail.

As we learned Joe Dixon's interpretation of trail signs, and as we, ourselves, became more keen observers, we grew more efficient in reading the wayside and the autographs we found there. [*Ruth Moore*, YOSEMITE SCHOOL OF FIELD NATURAL HISTORY YEARBOOK (1934) 163-164.]

CONSTANCE GORDON-CUMMING
*Digger Indians, Yosemite*, 1878
Watercolor
Yosemite Collection

# 2 MONOLITHS

IN ORDER TO UNDERSTAND PEOPLE'S REACTIONS to the great domes of Yosemite, it is necessary, first and foremost, to realize that the domes are alive. Ludlow, standing on Old Inspiration Point and surveying the scene in front of him, had this to say about Half Dome, whose Indian name was Tis-sa-ack:

> The glory of this southern wall comes at the termination of our view opposite the North Dome. Here the precipice rises to the height of nearly one sheer mile with a parabolic sky-line, and its posterior surface is as elegantly rounded as an acorn-cup. From this contour results a naked semi-cone of polished granite, whose face would cover one of our smaller Eastern counties, though its exquisite proportions make it seem a thing to hold in the hollow of the hand. A small pine-covered *glacis* of detritus lies at its foot, but every yard above that is bare of all life save the palaeozoic memories which have wrinkled the granite Colossus from the earliest seethings of the fire-time. I never could call a Yo-Semite crag *inorganic*, as I used to speak of everything not strictly animal or vegetal. In the presence of the Great South Dome [Half Dome] that utterance became blasphemous. Not living was it: Who knew but the *debris* at its foot was merely the cast-off sweat and *exuviae* of a stone life's great work-day? Who knew but the vital changes which were going on within its gritty cellular tissue were only imperceptible to us because silent and vastly secular? What was he who stood up before Tis-sa-ack and said, "Thou art dead rock!" save a momentary sojourner in the bosom of a cyclic period whose clock his race had never yet lived long enough to hear strike? What, too, if Tis-sa-ack himself were but one of the atoms in a grand organism where we could see only by monads at a time, —if he and the sun and the sea were but cells or organs of some one small being in the fenceless *vivarium* of the Universe? Let not the ephemeron that lights on a baby's hand generalize too rashly upon the non-growing of organisms! As we thought on these things, we bared our heads to the barer forehead of Tis-sa-ack. [*Ludlow, "Seven Weeks,"* 747.]

A few years later Muir seconded this point of view:

> I had more magnificent views of the upper mountains, and of the great South Dome, said to be the grandest rock in the world. Well it may be, since it is of such noble dimensions and sculpture.

A wonderfully impressive monument, its lines exquisite in fineness, and though sublime in size, is finished like the finest work of art, and seems to be alive. [*Muir*, MY FIRST SUMMER, *122.*]

The Ahwahnichis, long before Ludlow and Muir, associated El Capitan and Half Dome with their legendary heroes, thus initiating the process of endowing these great rocks with human characteristics. What follows is an abridged version of the story of Tu-tok-a-nu-la and Tis-sa-ack:

It has been a long time since The Great Spirit led a band of his favorite children into the mountains, this beautiful Valley of Ah-wah-nee. They were happy, and multiplied, and prospered and became a great nation. Their chief had a little son which made him very happy. When he grew to manhood, he was a chief and beloved leader of all his people. His people prepared him a lofty throne on the crown of the great rock which guards The Gateway of the Valley, and he was called Tu-tok-a-nu-la, after the great cranes that lived in the meadow near the top. From his high rocky throne he kept watch over the Valley and the people whom he loved.

One day as Tu-tok-a-nu-la sat gazing into the glowing colors of the west, he saw approaching his Valley a strange people, led by a maiden of exceptional beauty and loveliness. He called to them and the maiden answered him, saying, "It is I, Tis-sa-ack. We have heard of the great and good chief, Tu-tok-a-nu-la, of his great people and his wonderful Valley. We bring presents of baskets and beads and skins. After we have rested we will return to my people in the far south." Tu-tok-a-nu-la welcomed the visitors from the land to the south and had prepared for them a home on the summit of the great dome at the eastern end of the Valley. Tu-tok-a-nu-la visited her often in her mountain home. He was charmed by her wonderful beauty and sweetness, and begged her to stay and become his wife, but she denied him, saying, "No, I must soon return with my people to their home in the far south." And when Tu-tok-a-nu-la became importunate in his wooing, she left her home in the night and was never seen again.

When the great chief knew that she was gone, a terrible loneliness and sorrow came to him, and he wandered away through the forests in search of her, forgetting his people in Ah-wah-nee. He forgot to call upon the Great Spirit to send the timely rains. So great was his neglect that the streams grew smaller and finally became dry. The crops failed. The hunters came back from the forests without meat, and the fishermen returned from the streams empty-handed.

The Great Spirit became very angry with Tu-tok-a-nu-la. The earth trembled with his wrath so that the rocks fell down into the Valley from the surrounding cliffs. The great dome that had been the home of Tis-sa-ack was destroyed and half of it fell into the Valley. The melting snows from the high mountains came down into the Valley in a flood and drowned hundreds of people. But the wrath of the Great Spirit was quickly spent, and the heavens grew quiet again. The floods receded, the sun shone, and once more peace and calm reigned over Ah-wah-nee.

And, when the Valley was once again clothed in beauty and plenty, there appeared on the broken face of the dome which had been her home, the beautiful face of Tis-sa-ack, where it can still be seen to this day. And the dome was named Tis-sa-ack, in memory of the fair visitor who had been loved by all the people of Ah-wah-nee. At the same time, that all might hold his memory in their hearts, there appeared on the face of the great rock supporting his throne, the magestic figure of the great chief, dressed in a flowing robe and pointing a finger to where he had gone, to El-o-win, the happy land beyond the setting sun. [LEGENDS OF THE YOSEMITE MIWOK *(1981) 37-38.*]

Albert Richardson and Josiah Whitney also saw in the lines and shape of El Capitan the features of an indomitable chieftain:

El Capitan is grandest of all. No tuft of beard shades or fringes its closely shaven face. No tenacious vine even can fasten its tendrils, to climb that smooth, seamless, stupendous wall. There it will stand, grandeur, massiveness, indestructibility, till the heavens shall pass away with a great noise, and the elements melt with fervent heat. [*Albert D. Richardson*, BEYOND THE MISSISSIPPI *(1867) 426.*]

El Capitan imposes on us by its stupendous bulk, which seems as if hewed from the mountains on purpose to stand as the type of eternal massiveness. [*J. D. Whitney*, THE YOSEMITE BOOK *(1868) 56.*]

Remarks about the personality of Half Dome center on state of mind, perhaps in keeping with the perception that El Capitan is an upright figure while Half Dome is head and shoulders:

From a point close by one may gain a fine view of the chief glory of the valley, the Half Dome, the loftiest, most sublime and at the same time most impressive and beautiful of all the rocky sentinels that guard this abode of glory. Rising over 4,750 feet above the floor, where all is clothed in richest verdure, its face sculptured by Time and Storm, Glacier and Frost, while its head is smoothed to graceful curves, it is poised in calm, serene majesty. [*George Wharton James*, CALIFORNIA ROMANTIC AND BEAUTIFUL *(1914) 225.*]

To me, Half Dome is not a static, inorganic object: it is alive with vibrant significance, constantly changing in every aspect of its appearance and mood with the time of the day, the season of the year, and the position of the viewer. I have been fascinated by its various essences and appearances. From Mirror Lake it is an overpowering mass; from Glacier Point it is a soaring, proud dome; from Sentinel Bridge it is majestic and serene. [*Goldstein*, THE MAGNIFICENT WEST: YOSEMITE *(1973) 5, 19.*]

Yonder stands the South Dome, its crown high above our camp, though its base is four thousand feet below us; a most noble rock, it seems full of thought, clothed with living light, no sense of dead stone about it, all spiritualized, neither heavy looking nor light, steadfast in serene strength like a god. [*Muir*, MY FIRST SUMMER, *129.*]

Both El Capitan and Half Dome have reached a height human beings profoundly yearn for but seem never to attain no matter how high and hard they climb: a spiritual state of mind of complete self-acceptance. Only by such a supposition can we account for the constant reiteration in the passages quoted above of the idea of serenity. For Ludlow, El Capitan is no less than a granite Buddha:

> Our eyes seemed spellbound to the tremendous precipice which stood smiling, not frowning at us, in all the serene radiance of a snow-white granite Boodha,—broadly burning, rather than glistening, in the white-hot splendors of the setting sun. [*Ludlow, "Seven Weeks," 746.*]

Like the character of Yosemite as a whole, as we have seen in Chapter One, the personalities of its domes are more complicated and problematic than the above statements would lead us to believe. For Greeley, El Capitan has a spirituality all right, but it is a strange and unsettling one. He is standing at midnight in the Gateway, the area at the western end of Bridal Veil Meadow, looking east at El Capitan:

> That first full, deliberate gaze up the opposite height! can I ever forget it? The valley is here scarcely half a mile wide, while its northern wall of mainly naked, perpendicular granite is at least 4,000 feet high—probably more. But the modicum of moonlight that fell into this awful gorge gave to that precipice a vagueness of outline, an indefinite vastness, a ghostly and weird spirituality. Had the mountain spoken to me in audible voice, or begun to lean over with the purpose of burying me beneath its crushing mass, I should hardly have been surprised. [*Greeley*, NEW YORK TRIBUNE *(1859).*]

Many other commentators intuitively sense the darker side of the personalities of both El Capitan and Half Dome. They feel watched, frowned upon, and generally menaced:

> Nearly opposite to the Bridal Veil stands the Monarch of the Vale, the El Capitan of the Yosemite Tribe. It is the terminus of a ridge of mountains standing out in bold relief, with perpendicular front, and rising to an elevation of 3,100 feet above the level of the river that roars at his base. His stern and prominent front is the first to greet the eye of the visitor. He almost seemed to frown on us as we passed near his base. [*William Baer, "A Trip to the Yosemite Falls" (1856).*]

> Whether on the highest peak or in the valley, the face of El Capitan seems to follow and haunt you. [*Hunt, "California Letters" (1893).*]

GEORGE TIRRELL
[*Nevada Fall and Liberty Cap*], 1858
Pencil and white chalk on paper
Yosemite Collection

GEORGE BAKER
*South Dome, Liberty Cap, and Nevada Fall*, no date
Handcolored lithograph
Yosemite Collection

Behind us frowned the Tutochanulah, great shadows flitting across his grizzled front as he seemed meditating upon the propriety of toppling over and engulfing us. [*James H. Lawrence, "Discovery of the Nevada Fall" (1884) 367.*]

After looking up at the terrible To-coy-ae [North Dome] and Tis-sa-ack, bald granite domes four and five thousand feet high, after following the line of overlapping arches and columns and peaks of stone; high up in the air on either hand as far as you can see, seeming to tower and grow, and threaten to topple under your very gaze,—there is a sense of protection in the neighborhood of an azalea, a new comradeship with a daisy. They have summered and wintered in Ah-wah-ne, and are not afraid. [*Helen Hunt Jackson*, AH-WAH-NE DAYS *(1872) 49.*]

The apparent threat from El Capitan is simply too much for one visitor to stomach:

At Inspiration Point we stopped and took in the scene as far as possible; all in our carriage were carried away with the grandeur of the El Capitan Rock. Hargrove said it made him sick and turned his head away. [*"Bound for Yosemite" (1896).*]

Perhaps it is this feeling of disaster about to happen, that caused so many of the early speculations about the origin of the valley to emphasize violence and catastrophe:

I beheld a half-dome of rock, one mile high. Originally a vast granite mountain, it was riven from top to bottom by some ancient convulsion, which cleft asunder the everlasting hills and rent the great globe itself. [*Richardson*, BEYOND THE MISSISSIPPI *(1867) 421.*]

The shattered fronts of walls stand out sharp and terrible, sweeping down in broken crag and cliff to a valley whereon the shadow of autumnal death has left its solemnity. There is no longer an air of beauty. In this cold, naked strength, one has crowded on him the geological record of mountain work, of granite plateau suddenly rent asunder, of the slow, imperfect manner in which Nature has vainly striven to smooth her rough work and bury the ruins with thousands of years' accumulation of soil and *debris*. [*Clarence King*, MOUNTAINEERING IN THE SIERRA NEVADA *(1872) 134.*]

Its formation has been instantaneous—the mighty crash of a moment. Prof. J. D. Whitney says it has sunk; that the mass between the walls (originally) has gone down to unknown depths; and the testimony of the walls goes to show that the theory is correct. Look across the valley, at the south wall, from Cathedral Rock to Glacier Point; the entire wall is a shattered mass, and sunk from the Sentinel Dome. Again, look from the head of the Yosemite Falls to the North Dome; you see the same traces of a violent rending force; look at the North Dome particularly; like the Sentinel Dome, it is only dome-shaped next to the valley, and has been formed the same way. Not so with the South Dome (local name of Half Dome); the strata has sunk away from all sides of it. [*John Conway*, TOURISTS' GUIDE FROM THE YOSEMITE VALLEY TO EAGLE PEAK *(1881) 6.*]

The personality of Yosemite's major domes is remarkably similar to the personality of God in the Judaeo-Christian tradition. It is hardly surprising, therefore, to find that those stone features are frequently given the functions of gods and treated as objects of worship. In the following passage Wilson summarizes the godlike traits of El Capitan and has "him" keep watch over us and bless us:

> Towering over thirty-six hundred feet above the Valley floor, the world's largest and highest rock, the world's most nearly perpendicular cliff, embracing on its surface over three hundred and twenty acres of glacier-worn, storm-beaten solid granite, the unspeakable grandeur, the preeminent glory and strength, the air of unutterable age, irresistible power, and infinite repose of El Capitan beggar description. Here this great "rock chief" stands, the mightiest, the most glorious of his kind, keeping perpetual vigil over the rock portals of his kingdom, and we can but bow our heads in reverent awe to receive the benediction which he bestows upon all who pass his throne. [*Wilson*, THE LORE AND THE LURE OF YOSEMITE *(1928) 34.*]

Robert Sterling Yard wrote a fictionalized account of a trip to the major National Parks by the standardized American family of four. He humorously depicts Half Dome as the all-knowing giver of gifts:

> In the morning, Margaret would say she wanted steak for lunch, and in a little while a boy would walk in with the steak.
>
> "It's like the Arabian Nights," Margaret would say. "You are the fairy, Mother."
>
> Jack teased to know how Mrs. Jefferson brought about this magic. How did the shops in the village know what she wanted?
>
> "I just wave my hands to old Half Dome up there, and whisper what I want," said Mrs. Jefferson, "and, presto, it is here."
>
> "How lovely!" cried Margaret, clapping her hands.
>
> "Mother's just fooling us," said Jack, "and I'm going to find out how she does it."
>
> "Please don't, Jack," pleaded Margaret. "I don't want to know. I'd rather think it is old Half Dome sends us the things we want." [*Robert Sterling Yard*, TOP OF THE CONTINENT: STORY OF A CHEERFUL JOURNEY THROUGH OUR NATIONAL PARKS *(1917) 166.*]

Both Wilson and Yard are too deeply committed to a Judaeo-Christian spiritual monotheism to really believe that stone monoliths are gods. Wilson makes this point explicitly in writing about Half Dome:

> Keeping watch over the rear of the Valley, even as El Capitan guards The Gateway, the ponderous immobility of this monster of granite inspires a feeling which defies analysis. From everywhere in the upper end of the Valley the eye is constantly drawn back to its impressive bulk, and who can doubt that if we were given to the practice of endowing with the personality and powers of a Deity

inanimate objects of stone and wood, this inexpressibly sublime mountain would now be an object of worship. [*Wilson,* THE LORE AND THE LURE OF YOSEMITE *(1928) 43.*]

Nevertheless, the following two authors seem very close to passing over the border separating make-believe from belief. Hannah Davidson notes that both the Greeks and the Jews located their gods in nearby mountains. Apparently she has found her own strong-armed god in the mountains of California, who mystically gathers up her individuality in his own. The fear that Moses felt on Mt. Sinai seizes her; like him she is about to see her god of hosts face to face:

> The Greeks set the dwelling place of Jove among the mountains. Jehovah, the Lawgiver spoke to the Jews from the clouds and darkness around their tops; His footsteps are on the hills but His habitation is on the mountains.
>
> Up the last long hill before Inspiration Point we all walked, a few steps forward at a time, and a great many upward and around on the narrrow mountain road overhanging the gorge. Even now my heart beats & my breath comes quick remembering the awful sublimity of that walk & those scenes. Our individuality was swallowed up. We scarcely knew that we were.
>
> As we rounded the last shoulder of the great wall that all day had reared itself between us and Yosemite our hearts beat fast almost with fear to catch the first glimpse of what we had come so far to see.
>
> We came to a great mass of rock and earth & trees that seemed to overhang the gorge below us. We pushed our way out onto it as far as we dared & then looked around. The valley lay so far below that we could not see the river nor hear its noisy rushing over its rocky bed. At the left was outspread the same wonderful green walled canyon we had seen an hour before; we turned around: at the right there arose in the distance a sheer towering mass of white granite, fronting a dark shadowy cliff. We were in the presence of El Capitan & Cathedral Rocks, the Gates of Yosemite. Through them strange white masses beckoned & withdrew: the evening light lay in sunshine on the one side, in shadow on the other. El Capitan seemed the leader of a host, he lifted his awful brow 6000 ft in air and beckoned us over; it was but a step: the tiny birds rested on his head, the mountain snows trickled down his face, the pine & the manzanniia [sic] found a resting place on his shoulder, why not we! All in good time, El Capitan, Man's footsteps lie across thy breast & thy arms are strong. [*Hannah Amelia Noyes Davidson, "Nannie's Description of Yosemite Valley" (1885).*]

Herbert Jump not only compares El Capitan with God but also draws an extended analogy between it and the second person of the Christian Trinity:

> Of all the heights that make the Valley incomparable, El Capitan is the most unforgettable. And there is no one of us but supposes his knowledge of Spanish to be sufficient for translating the name. I was told, however, a while ago, that the popular translation was quite inadequate.

"El Capitan," according to my informant, was the title given by the old padres to God. What was done, therefore, sometime in the undefined past, was the splendidly daring thing of naming this stupendous cliff with the very name of the Almighty! How true the poetry of it! How fitting the suggestion! "God" ushers us into the temple of the Yosemite. "God" is our first impression upon coming in, our last impression on going out.

For me personally another and most helpful mental assocation has come to pass. El Capitan is to me not so much a symbol of God as a symbol of Christ, God revealed in man. In that unrivalled wall of granite, ascending perpendicularly three thousand feet above the beholder, I seem to see humanity at its height, my own soul raised to its divinest potencies in Jesus. The heights of the Yosemite lead me to God, but they lead me thither by way of the God-man. El Capitan is my Captain, "the captain of my salvation," the Christ.

When the sad day arrives that compels a farewell to the gray rocks and the white waters, the green meadows and the rainbow-tinted flowers,—as your conveyance slips down the Valley toward El Portal and the problems of life, perform for the sake of your soul this little ritual of affection:

Look backward once again toward the ineffable kingly dignity of El Capitan. In that brave front of granite, high-browed and erect toward the sun, see with your imagination's eye a picture of the Christ, challenging, inspiring, dominating, commanding you. See Him urging you into the thick of things with an apostolic commission to help bring His strength and purity into the world's life. See Him boldly summoning you to join Him in resistance to all cheap compromise, all convenient insincerity, all lazy cowardice that masquerades under the name of tact. See Him inviting you to share His patience, His long-suffering beneath the battering storms, His calm and unapologetic faith in the final invincibility of truth. See Him, the eternal, self-giving Christ, rooted deep in the earth but stretching His aspiring height toward the skies,—the union of the seer and the man of affairs, the fusion of the dreamer and the soldier. If thus, as you leave the Valley, the El Capitan Christ dismisses you with His blessing and His imperative, then you will bring into the everyday world a spiritual message from the Yosemite. You will become indeed a mountain soul. [*Herbert Jump*, THE YOSEMITE: A SPIRITUAL INTERPRETATION *(1916) 21-24, 33-35.*]

CHARLES DORMAN ROBINSON
*Twin Regalities*, no date
Oil on canvas
Yosemite Collection

Thomas Moran
[*Bridal Veil Fall*], no date
Oil on canvas (unfinished)
Yosemite Collection

# 3 WATERFALLS

## *Bridal Veil Fall*

> *So out of the ground the Lord God formed every beast of the field and every bird of the air, and brought them to the man to see what he would call them; and whatever the man called every living creature, that was its name.* [GENESIS 3:19]

WHITE ADVENTURERS ENTERING YOSEMITE IN THE 1850s had the opportunity to play Adam, and they took advantage of it. Nowhere in Yosemite was the outcome of the naming game more important than with the waterfall opposite El Capitan. Its Miwok name is "Pohono," generally translated into English, especially in the nineteenth century, as "Spirit of the Evil Wind." Perhaps a more accurate rendering might be "Power Wind." Because fear is an important element in the reaction of so many park visitors, one would expect them to understand inituitively the appropriateness of the Miwok name. Instead they usually miss the point entirely:

> "Pohono" is the euphonious name given by the Yo Semite Indians to one of the most graceful of the many waterfalls found leaping the rim of that mountain walled valley. To the Indian it is the "Spirit of the Evil Wind," whose breath is blighting to health and fatal to life; as he passes it, a feeling of distress almost amounting to dread steals over him, and he hurries by it at the height of his speed; especially when above, as something to shun. Its beautiful and rainbow lighted mists have no charm to detain him; or its diamond studded folds and watery rockets to cause his footsteps to linger and his soul to admire. To his mind the voices of those who have sickened and died within its baneful circle are perpetually admonishing him to shun Pohono. The song it is constantly singing, no matter how sweet and entrancing would only be that of the Syren to his heart. No, Pohono, he dreads thee; all thy beauty cannot win his love or banish his superstitious fear. [*James Mason Hutchings*(?), YO SEMITE ASSEMBLY *(1877)*.]

The superstitious Indians called this waterfall "Pohono," meaning "evil spirit," and were frightened. How foolish of them. A mischievous waterfall perhaps, but certainly a gay and beautiful one, and well described by the name "Bridal Veil." [*Stanley Plumb*, FOUR SEASONS IN YOSEMITE NATIONAL PARK *(1936)*.]

KUCHEL AND DRESEL
*Bridal Veil Water Fall*, no date
Nagel, printer
E. Camerer, lithographer
Chromolithograph
Courtesy, Bancroft Library

Both Hutchings and Plumb make an understandable but fundamental mistake. They assume that beauty casts out fear. Finding no sensible basis for the Miwok's dread, they conclude it is the result of superstition. In reality the fear and, therefore, the name Pohono arise out of something profoundly unsettling about the power of moving water. Plumb was right about one thing, however: to the imagination of white Americans this waterfall is well described by the name "Bridal Veil." Several claimed to be the Adam who named it. Hutchings, writing in the 1880s, said he named it on his first visit in 1855:

> A few advancing footsteps brought us to the foot of a fall, whose charming presence had long challenged our admiration; and, as we stood watching the changing drapery of its watery folds, the silence was eventually broken by my remark, "Is it not as graceful, and as beautiful as the veil of a bride?" to which Mr. Ayres rejoined, "That is suggestive of a very pretty and most apposite name. I propose that we now baptize it, and call it, 'The Bridal Veil Fall,' as one that is both characteristic and euphonious." This was instantly concurred in by each of our party, and has since been so known, and called, by the general public. [*Hutchings*, IN THE HEART OF THE SIERRAS *(1886) 89.*]

Hutchings' propensity for self-aggrandizement and the fact that Thomas Ayres entitled his drawing of this fall "Cascade of the Rainbow" raises doubts about the accuracy of his account. William Baer, who entered Yosemite Valley the following year, was aware only of Ayres' appellation and believed that he was the first to call it Bridal Veil:

> Thus we rode along, glancing from summit to summit of towering rocks, until proceeding for about a mile and a half up stream, we came opposite the falls of what has been inappropriately called the Cascade of the Rainbow. We say this not to reflect upon the judgment of the gentleman who has ventured to bestow this fanciful name upon one of the most attractive cascades of the Valley. But inasmuch as the falls in the Valley are never of the magnitude of a cataract, and all reflect rainbows at certain hours of the day, the name might be promiscuously applied to all the cascades separately. Viewed from any quarter or point of the horizon, this cascade is very attractive. To our mind, it resembled a cambric veil, of ample folds, of the finest texture, the purest whiteness, and fringed with silver fleece or silken floss. Sitting beside the cherry trees, at some fifty yards from the falls, we were singularly struck with the graceful motion of the water in its descent, when pressed by the breeze. Its foldings and unfoldings—its wavings and its twistings—its contractings and expandings—possess an irresistibly attractive fascination, beyond any object of which we have ever gazed, and one, too, from which the eyes are drawn with the greatest reluctance. At night, when our trip recurs to our mind, we muse on its liveliness, until we again hear the noise of its waters in their fall, and see the rainbows that follow its wanderings through the air, in its downward search for the earth and the Valley. We make bold to call it the Bridal Veil; and those who may have the felicity to witness the stream floating

in the embrace of the morning breeze, will acknowledge the resemblance, and perhaps pardon the liberty we have taken in attempting to apply so poetical a name to this Queen of the Valley. [*Baer, "A Trip to the Yosemite Falls" (1856).*]

Veil brings a single image to mind, Bridal Veil an entire drama. Over the years writers have played out in their prose almost every conceivable act of this drama, from rejected suitors to blushing courtship and regal marriage. Bridal Veil shyly hides her beauty from the gaze of the ordinary men who come to visit her:

> The feeling of awe, wonder, and admiration—almost amounting to adoration—that thrilled our very souls, it is impossible to portray, as we looked upon this enchanting scene. The gracefully undulating and wavy sheets of spray that fell in gauze-like and ethereal folds; now expanding, now contracting; now glittering in the sunlight, like a veil of diamonds; now changed into one vast many-colored cloud, that threw its misty drapery over the falling torrent, as if in very modesty, to veil its unspeakable beauty from our too eagerly admiring sight. [*Hutchings, "The Great Yo-Semite Valley" (1859-60) 242.*]

When anyone other than her betrothed makes rude advances, she is saved by a comforting father:

> The storm king took his departure on the evening of the 16th. The hoary headed old bachelor played the virgin real mean the past Winter. He has stuck right by her, making love to her—dressing her from top to toe in glittering icicles of the largest size. No wonder the poor dear thought he meant something this time. However, like most other virgins in trouble, she has been comforted. The next morning after his departure old Sol clasped her in his warm embrace and soothed her into a flood of tears; and oh, what tears,—only such as the Yo Semite virgin can shed—hundreds of tears in solid masses, making the Valley tremble. [*John Conway, "Letter from Yo Semite" (1874).*]

Her intended is El Capitan, naturally enough, who lives just across the valley. One day he will lead her to Cathedral Rock where they will join in holy matrimony:

> It does not require a great stretch of imagination to picture the grim old Spanish Captain sternly waiting for his reluctant bride to dry the flood of crocodile-tears young ladies sometimes see fit to dispense on such occasions, and to lead her to the Cathedral, still further up the valley, while the giant pines stand in whispering ranks to see the ceremony, and the setting sun places a tiara of prismatic gems among the feathery plumes on the maiden's head as its wedding-gift. [*Dodd,* SUMMER SAUNTERINGS *(1882) 110.*]

Old men, of course, are relegated to the role of spectators, but even so watching the bride show off her veils makes them feel young again:

There is considerable breeze to-day; and now, while I write, the Bride's veil is wafted from side to side, and sometimes lifted until I can almost see the blushing face of the Bride herself—the beautiful spirit of the fall. But whose bride? Is it old El Capitan? Strength and grandeur united with grace and beauty! Fitting union!

At 3 P.M. went again alone to the lower side of the meadow and sat down before the gate of the valley. From this point I look directly through the gate and up the valley. There again, rising to the very skies, stands the huge mass of El Capitan on one side, and on the other the towering peak of the Cathedral, with the Veiled Bride retiring a little back from the too ardent gaze of admiration. The sky is perfectly serene, except heavy masses of snow-white cumulus, sharply defined against the deep blue of the sky, filling the space beyond the gate. The wavy motion of the Bride's veil, as I gaze steadfastly upon it, drowses my sense; I sit in a kind of delicious dream, the scenery unconsciously mingling with my dream.

Five P.M. Went, all of us, this afternoon to visit the Bride. Saw again the glorious crown set by the sun upon her beautiful head. Swam in the pool at her feet. Tried to get a peep beneath the veil, but got pelted beyond endurance with water-drops, by the little fairies which guard her beauty, for my sacrilegious rudeness. Nevertheless, came back much exhilarated, and feeling more like a boy than I had felt for many, many years. [*Joseph LeConte*, A JOURNAL OF RAMBLINGS (*1875*) *64, 65.*]

## Yosemite Falls

BRIDAL VEIL FALL is an actor in the drama of love and marriage. Yosemite Falls enact another basic human drama: the journey from youth through suffering (and sometimes death) to resurrection and renewal. In telling this story writers rarely miss an opportunity to pun on the name of the river that receives Yosemite Creek:

> The waters, waked from their winter sleep into fulness of life, come dancing down the distant slopes —the merry "laughter of the mountains"—and racing along the canyon until reaching the precipice, then impetuously leaping over the lip of massive granite, they break into an "avalanche of snowy rockets," chasing each other wildly down the plunge, finally falling far below into a rocky basin with the roar of a battle-field. Pausing here a moment, as if to recover breath, they start again in the race, but this time more cautiously in the cascades; suddenly, stirred by the old spirit, they make a final leap; then, like the chastened sons of sorrow, wise from the things they have suffered, they flow quietly on to mingle with the waters of the Merced. [*William Wilson Ross*, 10,000 MILES BY LAND AND SEA (*1876*) *222-223.*]

For the most vivid expressions of the theme of journey, we must turn to Yosemite's poets:

*In what far angel-haunted spring*
    *Hast thou, fair stream, thy happy birth?*
*What is thy will that thou shouldst fling*
    *Thy slender form from Heaven to earth?*

*Forever falling, and to fall*
    *Forever from that cloudy gate,*
*And crying with incessant call*
    *Against the tumult of thy fate.*

*The valley takes thee, trembling stream,*
    *In smoky fragments on its breast;*
*Wake, giddy leaper, from thy dream.*
    *Here is at last some peaceful rest.*

[from *Charles Warren Stoddard, "Yo-Semite Falls" (1867).*]

*A burst of molten silver, born*
    *Of mountain snow,*
*That bears the beauty of the morn*
    *Within its flow.*

*A wave of streaming white that falls,*
    *And, falling, flings*
*Against the gray old granite walls*
    *Its silver wings.*

*A whitened fire from out the sky,*
    *Whose arrowed strands*
*In sunlight gleam and flash and die,*
    *Like earth-hurled brands.*

*A river turned to cloud mist, blown*
    *By every breath,*
*Yet coming to its crystal own,*
    *After death.*

[from *Harold Symmes, "Cloud Mist: Yosemite Falls" (1911).*]

From the beginning, writers have also seen the flow of water over Yosemite Falls as symbolic of the cycles of nature. Not surprisingly, many of the early statements of this theme are in terms of divine providence:

So the Almighty sets the forces of nature to grinding the solid granite into flour for human food,—the "River of Mercy" wafting it out upon the meadows, to be transmuted by golden sunlight and nightly dews into ripened wheat and purpling grapes. [*Coffin*, OUR NEW WAY ROUND THE WORLD (*1869*) *488-489.*]

John Muir gave this theme its clearest expression in secular terms:

Contemplating the lace-like fabric of streams outspread over the mountains, we are reminded that everything is flowing—going somewhere, animals and so-called lifeless rocks as well as water. Thus the snow flows fast or slow in grand beauty-making glaciers and avalanches; the air in majestic floods carrying minerals, plant leaves, seeds, spores, with streams of music and fragrance; water streams carrying rocks both in solution and in the form of mud particles, sand, pebbles, and boulders. Rocks flow from volcanoes like water from springs, and animals flock together and flow in currents modified by stepping, leaping, gliding, flying, swimming, etc. While the stars go streaming through space pulsed on and on forever like blood globules in Nature's warm heart. [*Muir*, MY FIRST SUMMER (*1911*) *236.*]

In our own time Gary Snyder has turned Muir's vision into poetry. Like Stoddard and Symmes he begins by imagining the birth of Yosemite Creek in melting snow. Its leap over rock ledge reminds him of the complete circle water makes from precipitation to evaporation and back again, and of the role the uplifted Sierra Nevada plays in Yosemite weather. What happens in the park is, however, only an instance of what happens worldwide, for the mind of nature thinks in ever-repeating circles. In this moving drama only the rainbow and the poet stand still:

I meditated by the falls from different angles. I had just finished writing a poem about the water cycle in the Sierra Nevada, so I was full of thinking in those metaphors. And so the [following] poem just came. I was moved very deeply to actually pray somehow by being there:

> *Over stone lip*
> *the creek leaps out as one*
> *divides in spray and streamers,*
> *lets it all: go.*
>
> *Above, back there, the snowfields,*
> *rocked between granite ribs*
> *turn spongy in the summer sun*
> *water slips out under*
> *mucky shallow flows*
> *enmeshed with roots of flower & moss & heather*

*seeps through swampy meadow*
*gathers to shimmer sandy shiny flats*
*then soars off ledges—*

*Crash and thunder on the boulders at the base.*
*painless, playing,*
*droplets regather*
*seek the lowest, and keep going down.*
*in gravelly beds.*

*There is no use, the water cycle tumbles round—*

*Sierra Nevada*
*could lift the heart so high*
*fault block uplift*
*thrust of westward slipping crust—one way*
*to raise and swing the clouds around—*
*thus pine trees leapfrog up on sunlight*
*trapped in cells of leaf—*
*nutrient minerals called together*
*like a magic song*
*to lead a cedar log along, that hopes*
*to get to sea at last, a great canoe.*

*A soft breath, world-wide, of night and day.*
*rising, falling,*

*The Great Mind passes by its own*
*fine-honed thoughts,*
*going each way.*

*Rainbow hanging steady*
*only slightly wavering with the*
*swing of the whole spill*
*between the rising and the falling,*
*stands still.*

*I stand drenched in crashing spray and mist,*
*and pray.*

*[Gary Snyder, "Yosemite Falls" (1981-82).]*

## Vernal Fall

EVER SINCE the stairs beside Vernal Fall were completed about 1857, the experience of being drenched by rainbows on the Mist Trail has been the highlight of a climb up the Merced River Canyon. Particularly impressive is the seemingly miraculous coalescence of round rainbows out of the enveloping wind-blown spray:

> Rainbows of dazzling brightness shine at its base. Others of the party reported many; my own eyes, defective as to colors, beheld only two. But afterward when alone, I saw what to Hebrew prophet had been a vision of heaven, or the visible presence of the Almighty. It was the round rainbow—the complete circle. In the afternoon sun I stood upon a rock a hundred feet from the base of the fall, and nearly on a level with it. There were two brilliant rainbows of usual form—the crescent, the bow proper. But while I looked, the two horns of the inner or lower crescent suddenly lengthened, extending on each side to my feet—an entire circle, perfect as a finger-ring. In two or three seconds it passed away, shrinking to the first dimensions. Ten minutes later it formed again; and again as suddenly disappeared. Every sharp gust of wind showering the spray over me revealed for a moment the round rainbow. Completely drenched I stood for an hour and a half; and saw, fully twenty times, that dazzling circle of violet and gold, on a groundwork of wet dark rock, gay dripping flowers and vivid grass. I never looked upon any other scene in Nature so beautiful and impressive. [*Richardson*, BEYOND THE MISSISSIPPI *(1867) 428.*]

These circular rainbows wrap climbers in a mystical union with nature:

> You do not want any more descriptions I am sure, even of Vernal Falls, so I will only stop to tell you about the rainbows. At the foot of the falls, every particle of water is broken into atoms, and every atom catches a ray of light & dances the dizziest waltz with it, then starts off in a dozen directions at once & comes back & starts over a dozen times. When these fairy water drops at last escape, they rush right into the sunshine & are transfigured. One bow lies inside another circling the foot of the falls, even spanning the air above with roseate dripping fingers.
>
> We found a small corner out of the spray close to one side of the falls, just the right place to fill your eyes with seeing, & your ears with hearing. We were all alone with ourselves & the falls, & the sense of time, of space, of ourselves dropped away from us; we seemed to see pure, endless, boundless, free nature, and it spoke to us, without the intervention of signs. How long one seems to have been gone when one returns to ordinary affairs from such a trance. It is as if the soul had been free from the body for a little while. [*Davidson, "Nannie's Description of Yosemite Valley" (1885).*]

You do not have to search for the mythical land of delight that lies at the end of the rainbow. It comes to you:

No need here to travel for the magic rainbow end, where the money lies. It follows you, it trips you up, it tangles itself around your feet. As I first walked back toward the Fall, after going as far out in the spray as I dared, I accidentally slipped on a rolling stone. I looked down quickly, to find a firmer footing; and I looked down upon a broad band of the most brilliant rainbow. I exclaimed at the sight; but, as I exclaimed, the rainbow slipped to the left, then as I advanced it slowly retreated, as if luring me to the Fall. Suddenly as it came it vanished, on the surface of a wet boulder. A step or two back into the spray, and it danced under my feet; a step or two forward, and it was gone.

"These ain't any thing," said Murphy [Jackson's guide]. "The place where you get the rainbows is down there," pointing into what looked like the mouth of a steaming cauldron, some rods down the canyon.

Through this we must go if we walked down to Lady Franklin's Rock. Remembering the choked breath and dripping hair of the people seen the day before, we hesitated; but, remembering also the joy which flashed in their eyes, we longed.

"It's pretty bad now," said Murphy, reflectively. "Dunno's I've ever taken anybody through when the river was higher. But you're pretty sure-footed. I guess you'd git along well enough. An' ye won't never be sorry ye did it. I can tell ye that."

Never, indeed! Only sorry that I cannot remember it more vividly. Leaping from stone to stone, posing on slippery logs under water, clinging to Murphy's hand as to a life-preserver, blinded, choked, stifled, drenched, down into that canyon, through that steaming spray, we went. It was impossible to keep one's eyes open wide for more than half a second at a time. The spray drove and pelted, making great gusts of wind by its own weight as it fell. It seemed to whirl round and round, and wrap us, as if trying to draw us down into the black depths. It was desperately uncomfortable, and dangerous, no doubt. But what of that? We were taken into the heart of a carnival of light. Rainbows rioted everywhere, and we were crowding and jostling through as we could. The air was full of them, the ground danced with them, they climbed and chased and tumbled mockingly over our heads and shoulders, and across our faces. I nearly lost my footing, laughing at one, made chiefly of blue and purple, which flitted across Murphy's left eyebrow. They wheeled and broke into bits and flew; they swung and revolved and twined. When I looked at them in the air, I could think of nothing but a gigantic loom, on which threads of rainbow were being shuttled and woven with magic swiftness. When I looked down into the confusion of dark boulders and pools under our feet, I could think of nothing but gigantic millhoppers spinning round, and grinding up purple and blue and yellow and green and red. I held out my hand and caught the threads in the loom,—stopped them, turned them, snapped them. I leaned down and dipped into the purple and blue and yellow and green and red, and lifted them in the hollow of my palm. I do not think anybody could have come nearer to the secrets of rainbows if he had sat in the sky and watched the first one made. [*Jackson*, AH-WAH-NE DAYS *(1872) 56-58.*]

Kɪᴄʜᴇʟ ᴀɴᴅ Dʀᴇsᴇʟ
*Vernal Falls*, no date
Nagel, printer
Drawn from nature by E. Camerer
Chromolithograph
Courtesy, Bancroft Library

One writer, apparently having passed by the rainbow door to the land of fulfillment, contemplated the rather more drastic step of gaining entrance by going over the fall itself:

> Presently we came to the head of the rock, over which flows the Vernal. I have never seen such a gorgeous and imposing effect produced by water.
>
> We see water going smoothly over, over into the valley beneath, and a strange longing seizes one to throw oneself into its bosom, and be carried over with it, one knows not, cares not whither. You seem to think that it will take you to some other land, where your soul will find that something which every soul yearns after, and which none can define. [*William Minturn*, TRAVELS WEST *(1878) 267-268.*]

## *Nevada Fall*

NEVADA FALL has less written about it than any other major Yosemite landmark. Having spent their adjectives on Bridal Veil, Yosemite, and Vernal, writers are empty-mouthed by the time they arrive at the last and most inaccessible of the Valley's waterfalls. The comments that have been published make it clear that Nevada Fall is both beauty and beast. "To me it is the handsomest fall in the Yosemite," says Ridinghood in the *San Francisco Chronicle* of July 20, 1879, while Joseph LeConte is willing to include all the world's waterfalls in the comparison:

> The Nevada Fall is, I think, the grandest I have ever seen. The fall is six hundred to seven hundred feet high. It is not an absolutely perpendicular leap, like Vernal, but is all the grander on that account; as, by striking several ledges in its downward course, it is beaten into a volume of snowy spray, ever changing in form, and impossible to describe. From the same cause, too, it has a slight S-like curve which is exquisitely graceful. [*LeConte*, A JOURNAL OF RAMBLINGS *(1875) 54.*]

Hannah Davidson is willing to include all things on earth in the comparison:

> Nevada Falls is the most perfectly beautiful thing that I ever saw. The whole thing is like a vision, a picture rising right before you. It does not take you in and surround you at all, but there it is, there it was, & there you feel sure it will be just the same, if you should come a hundred times. [*Davidson, "Nannie's Description of Yosemite Valley" (1885).*]

Others portray it as anything but perfect and graceful:

> When the eye first glimpses Vernal Falls, one stops for quite a while to feast on its quiet, solemn, resistless majesty. It has such a calm and serene look, so different from Bridal Fall, Yosemite and

Illilouette. Its broad front, smooth and even, its outer waters lashed into foam, comes over in such a calm, dignified, stately fashion that it well represents an aged man's cultured brow, on which his white hair adds beauty as well as serene dignity.

A mile beyond is Nevada Fall, between six hundred and seven hundred feet high, whose waters are so dashed and churned and tossed about ere they are hurled over the lip that they are of a snowy whiteness. They come over in an entirely different fashion from those of Vernal. They seem hurried, almost apologetic, fluffy, fussy, nervous and agitated, so different, indeed, that it is hard to conceive the same water can so entirely change its character in the short mile before it appears as Vernal Fall. [*James*, CALIFORNIA ROMANTIC AND BEAUTIFUL *(1914)* 226.]

What fascinates people most about Nevada Fall is the terrible explosion of white water at its base:

From a projecting ledge, a sort of Table Rock, we were able to follow its mad leap down seven hundred feet, to look straight into the chasm where it was deepest and darkest, into the vortex of swirling, wrestling, fighting waters,—a mighty agony of contending forces, an image of eternal unrest. [*Greenwood*, NEW LIFE IN NEW LANDS *(1873) 345.*]

Yonder are Nevada Falls, plunging seven hundred feet, the water in arrows, the water in rockets, the water in pearls, the water in amethysts, the water in diamonds. That cascade flings down the rocks enough jewels to array all the earth in beauty, and rushes on until it drops into a very hell of waters, the smoke of their torment ascending forever and ever. [*T. De Witt Talmage, quoted in* THAT WONDERFUL COUNTRY: CALIFORNIA FOR PROFIT AND PLEASURE *(1890) 42.*]

HENRY PHLEFELD
[*People strolling around Tunnel Tree*]
From *Picturesque California*
Yosemite Collection

# 4 BIG TREES

## *Size*

SIZE IS WHAT FIRST IMPRESSES people about *Sequoiadendron gigantea*. Guidebooks typically approach the problem of communicating vastness to their readers by the straight and narrow path of listing actual measurements. In the excerpt that follows John Hittell assembles numbers so assiduously that he is almost unreadable:

> Seven miles by the wagon road from the Big Tree Hotel Station is the Mariposa Big Tree Grove, which for persons going to Yosemite, is the most conveniently accessible of all the groves of the *Sequoia gigantea*. It has 427 trees, the largest 34 feet through; 2, each of 33 feet; 13 between 25 and 32 feet; 36 between 20 and 25 feet; and 82 between 15 and 20 feet. The total number exceeding 15 feet in diameter is 134; and 293 are of smaller sizes, some not more than 2 feet through. The highest tree is 272 feet; and others have heights of 270, 268, 260, 256, 255, 250, 249, 244, 243, and 235, making 11 more than 230 feet high. The largest tree in circumference at the ground was 92½ feet; and others 91½, 89½, 87½, 86½, 82½, 82¼, 81½ and 81½, making 9 trees, each more than 80 feet in circumference at the ground. [BANCROFT'S PACIFIC COAST GUIDE BOOK *(1882) 177.*]

Such a passage fails utterly to communicate the feeling of size. After reading it one sympathizes with the writer of *Bancroft's Tourist's Guide*:

> Don't mention figures yet, please. When a man is overwhelmed with the sublime, don't plunge him into statistics. By and by, when we have cooled down to a safe pitch, we may condescend to hear the calm calculator project his inexorable mathematics into the very face of nature's sublimity and triumphantly tell us just *how* great this surpassing wonder is. But after all his exactest calculation, his absolute measurements and his positive assurances, one *feels* how small the fraction of real greatness which figures can express or the intellect apprehend. [*(1871) 45.*]

Because naked figures do little to warm the imagination, more inventive writers resort to comparisons, using the objects with which their readers are familiar. The Marquis de Beauvoir is writing for Parisians:

The "Grizzly," which is the finest, is thirty-six feet in diameter, and three hundred and sixty feet high, twice the height of the tower of St. Jacques! and higher than the cross on the dome of the Invalides! And the summit of the towers of Notre Dame might be sheltered under its lowest branch!

Thirty-six feet, if I mistake not, is a very good length for a ball-room in Paris. Fancy then a perfectly round room, one hundred and eight feet in circumference, hollowed out of a single tree, and the floor of this room made in one piece! Is not this wonderful? [*Beauvoir*, PEKIN, JEDDO, AND SAN FRANCISCO *(1872) 256-257.*]

Thomas Starr King's audience is the citizenry of Boston:

Was it possible that, before sunset, I was to stand by a living tree more than ninety feet in circuit, and over three hundred high? Think what these figures mean, my hasty reader, when transformed into solid bark and fibre. Take a ball of cord, measure off a hundred feet from it, cut it and tie the ends, and then by the aid of four or five companions stretch it into a circle, (if you have a parlor spacious enough to permit the experiment), and imagine that space filled with the column of a vigorous cedar. Now conceive this tree rooted on the Common near the Park Street entrance. What do you say to the idea of looking up its smooth trunk to a point higher than the topmost leaf of any elm on the Tremont Street mall, and of seeing then a bough thicker than the largest of those elms shooting out from it? What do you say to the fact that its plume would nod a hundred feet above the vane of Park Street spire? What do you say to the possibility, if it lay hollowed on the ground, of driving a barouche and four through it, without their being able to touch the highest point of its curved ceiling "with a ten foot pole"? If such a Colossus should spring near the frog pond, the old elm would look, by the side of it, like General Tom Thumb at the knee of Hercules. [*Thomas Starr King, "A Vacation among the Sierras" (January 12, 1861).*]

Human beings feel small in the presence of these trees. As one of the young boys puts it in William G. Paden's fantasy of a magic carpet ride through California, "Now I know just how a bug feels, crawling around in the grass." (*Seeing California* [1926] 108.) And the lesson the trees teach is the need for humility and silence:

As I stood in the stillness of that forest, as I mused a while there, I thought to myself what a wonderful thing it would be if all the people from New York could visit the big trees. There in front of me was a living thing to which I, in comparison, was but an ant. Yes, if I had my way, all the New Yorkers would be required to see this old forest—It would take all the conceit out of them. [*Dwight F. McKinney*, SEEING CALIFORNIA WITH HENERY *(1920) 12.*]

We drove on through the giant grove until we came to a tree in which a door had been cut for us to pass through. This was "Wawona," measuring twenty-eight feet in diameter. We drove into the tree, and stopped when our hind wheels were even with the tree. We had a four seated coach with four horses, and we were all inside of the tree but the heads of the leaders. On either side and above us were the red walls of the Cedar King, roughly hewn. We had nothing to say. [*Lilian Leland*, TRAVELING ALONE: A WOMAN'S JOURNEY AROUND THE WORLD *(1890) 328.*]

## Age

INTERESTINGLY ENOUGH, the great age of the Big Trees fascinates people more than does their size. Size is immediately present and visible. It may astound but it does not mystify. Age accumulates through the centuries inside the tree and requires an imaginative identification with the tree to "feel" it. The *Sequoia gigantea* seems to store up several thousand years of history and transport it not only into the present but into your presence. According to Emily Pfeiffer:

> These vast trees, bearing upon their charred rind the marks of scorching fires which might have been coeval with the siege of Jerusalem, were felt to unite our frail beings with the past, and to present to the imagination the procession of the ages, as a chain of which we were among the latest links. [*Emily Pfeiffer*, FLYING LEAVES FROM EAST AND WEST *(1885) 251.*]

Writers never tire of chronicling the events a giant Sequoia has lived through. Hundreds of paragraphs in effect complete the sentence, "It was alive when . . .":

> When the first feeling of astonishment at their enormous size has passed away, and we begin calmly to realize how venerable they are, how many years have gone to their building, then it is that we begin to appreciate the sight. Since their green fronds first peeped above the ground, what changes have come to mankind! Old faiths have died and new ones taken their place. The worship of Apis has ceased; the ibis and crocodiles of Nile are no longer sacred. The gods of Olympus have been dethroned; Venus, Passas, Mars, even Jove himself, faded away before a new dispensation. Jesus of Nazareth, born in a manger, brought to the world tidings of peace and great joy. Mahomet lived his strange life of vision, of toil and blood, to mould the faith of millions. Almost as now they stand they stood while Venice, Daughter of the Sea, rose from the rush-covered islands of the Adriatic, while she grew strong to crush the power of the Turks at Lepanto, and afterward spread the sails of her Argosies on every sea; while Florence lived through her short reign of power and glory; and as the Moors built the fairy towers of the Alhambra, that now for four hundred years have stood desolate on the hill of Darro. Even since they have grown old have the noblest achievements of our race been done. Bruno, Galileo, Copernicus, Kepler, Newton, have added to the simple knowledge of the

Chaldean shepherds all the wondrous stories of modern astronomy; Magna Charta been wrested from King John, and the printing press invented to disseminate knowledge into the humblest household. Since then Columbus, with genius and heroism, found for the development of mankind another hemisphere. There they have stood while war, superstition, ambition, dreams of liberty have swayed the hearts of men, and a better civilization been evolved from the decay of ancient faiths and empires. [*Alfred Lambourne*, PINE BRANCHES AND SEA WEEDS *(1889) 33-36.*]

Of course, the implicit corollary of the Sequoia's thousands is our own meagre four score and ten, a point not lost on Lambourne. He continues:

As the sun stoops low in the west and the evening shadows steal through the grove, we grow strangely quiet, do not care to talk or to ask questions of our guide; do not wish to know the name of this tree or that, but would rather listen to the whispering voices in the tree-tops far above, and watch the deepening of the red beams of twilight. The solemn presence of these last of a fading race is exerting its influence over us. How brief the sum of days allotted to human life! How like a meteor in the night, that glows and is gone, man's troubled existence! [*36.*]

The age of the giant Sequoias fascinates people not only because they have lived through so many of the crucial events of our civilization but because they appear immune to the ravages of time. Though wind and erosion eventually topple them, they so outlive us that they seem indestructible:

Of all the big trees of the Mariposa grove, and therefore of all the trees I have ever seen, the Grizzly Giant impressed me most profoundly; not, indeed, by its tallness or its symmetry, but by the hugeness of its cylindrical trunk, and by a certain gnarled grandeur, a fibrous, sinewy strength, which seems to defy time itself. [*LeConte*, A JOURNAL OF RAMBLINGS *(1875) 35.*]

Who that has seen them can think of them without having his blood tingle? Trees are now standing there that were old when Christ lived. These monarchs of foliage reigned before Caesar or Alexander; and the next thousand years will not shatter their scepter. They are the masts of the continent, their canvas spread on the winds while the old ship bears on its way through the ages. Their size, of which travelers speak, does not affect me so much as their longevity. Though so old now, the branches of some of them will crackle in the last conflagration of the planet. [*Talmage, quoted in* THAT WONDERFUL COUNTRY: CALIFORNIA FOR PROFIT AND PLEASURE *(1890) 41.*]

Fires have roared and blazed about them and burned their trunks and branches, and literally disembowelled some of them so that you can look up through them as through a tall chimney, but their upper branches are full of life, and green tufts of leaves crown their tops. The ice and snow of a thousand winters have wrapped them around in chilly embrace, and furious tempests have torn off immense limbs, but neither fire, nor frost, nor winter's furious storms, nor summer's glowing heat, have done aught but reveal their sturdy strength, their majestic and awe-inspiring character. They are the creations of One who is without beginning of days or end of life; and more than any living and growing thing that I have seen upon the face of the earth, they seem to partake of the divine element of unchanging and continuous existence. [*Charles Augustus Stoddard*, BEYOND THE ROCKIES; A SPRING JOURNEY IN CALIFORNIA *(1894) 132.*]

Perhaps it is this participation in divinity that causes some observers to treat giant Sequoias as gods:

They are woodland deities of such majestic presence and such serene beauty that you feel like falling at their feet and worshipping. [*Harriet Errington*, LETTERS AND JOURNAL FROM CALIFORNIA *1864-65, 53.*]

That they happen to be the tallest trees, the oldest trees, the most famous trees in the world is nowise the measure of my appreciation, for I lack the soul for record-breaking. My joy was rather that, looking up at them, I was in the Presence. I felt minded to remove my shoes. It was as if we all stood in the dim nave of some ancient cathedral reared ages before man worried the earth. I uncovered in their cold shadow as before the Holy of Holies. [*F. G. Aflalo*, SUNSET PLAYGROUNDS *(1909) 149.*]

A tree expresses the ancient idea of rebirth in its growth from a seed, hence the old Assyrian worship of a pine-cone. Every year a tree spreads out its ample foliage, as the sun in its power revivifies nature after the death of winter. In these forms a tree is a symbol of life, and of the life to be. It has still another aspect; it is a great object that moves. In its slight breath the tree whispers; as it increases, a louder rustle is heard; and, when the gale is strong, the branches move like the arms of some mighty Being, and loud are the sounds of its many leaves. According to the old ideas, the air, or wind, was the Spirit, or the Spirit of God; and a tree acting thus was looked upon as under the Divine afflatus. It was a thing which spoke, and which might be spoken to. In this we have the whole element of ancient worship, and the reason why Trees became Gods, and the Grove became a Temple. If I were a Tree Worshipper, and I sympathize with those who are, I would look upon the Big Trees of California as the great Gods of my system. [*Simpson*, MEETING THE SUN: A JOURNEY ALL ROUND THE WORLD *(1874) 387-388.*]

THOMAS AYRES
*Scene in the Valley of the Yohemity,* 1855
Black chalk on charcoal drawing on white paper
Yosemite Collection

# 5 EXITS

JOSEPH LECONTE NOTED that landscape affects us in two ways:

> There are two kinds of enjoyment of scenery, as of everything else. The one is the enjoyment of beauty and grandeur, heightened by novelty; the other is the enjoyment of the same mellowed and hallowed by association. The one affects more the imagination, the other the heart. [THE AUTOBIOGRAPHY OF JOSEPH LECONTE *(1903) 273.*]

No one knew Yosemite more by heart than Joseph LeConte himself. The author of *A Journal of Ramblings*, perhaps second only to Muir's *My First Summer in the Sierra* on the all-time Yosemite best books list, he came to the park repeatedly during the closing decades of the nineteenth century. As he grew older, he often wondered if the trip he was on would be his last:

> In June [1893] I went on a camping trip to the Yosemite with my son. I was far from well, and did not improve in the valley. Over three-score and ten, I felt that my life was spent, and thought that surely this was the last time I should see the Yosemite. Ill and low-spirited, I rode about alone, taking leave with tears of the splendid cliffs and glorious waterfalls as of dearest friends. [*LeConte*, AUTOBIOGRAPHY, *318.*]

After so long and rich an association with Yosemite, it was with sad but poetic justice that LeConte died in the valley eight years later. The procession carrying his body out of the valley in a rough-hewn coffin is one of the most moving of all Yosemite exits. Fortunately two accounts of this event are still extant, one a remembrance and the other a diary:

> It was a hot day in June 5, 1901, that I arrived by horse driven stage at Camp Curry in the Yosemite Valley. Camp Curry was then in its infancy and not many of the modern facilities of the present day were then in existence there. But, I liked it all the better for its rustic simplicity. We were quartered in tents with wooden floors and ate our meals in one dining tent. At night all the guests gathered around the camp fire and were entertained with jokes and nature stories pretty much as folks are at present, but this particular night we had the good fortune to hear a lecture by Joseph le Conte [sic],

Professor of Geology and Natural History at the University of California. A guest in camp who related his theory of the formation of this remarkable work of nature—the Yosemite Valley.

It was Professor le Conte's last lecture, for during the night the aged gentleman passed on quietly in the valley he so much loved. At that time facilities for taking care of the dead were very crude and limited. His friends hastily constructed a rustic coffin, lined it with ferns and cedar sprays and carefully wrapped the body in blankets so that it would not be bruised in its journey, which then required about three days to make the trip by horse driven stage over rough roads to Berkeley. The journey was begun at once and the stage traveled day and night so as to reach its destination in time for the funeral service in the Bay Region. [*William S. Rice, "A Yosemite Valley Reminiscence."*]

Bertha Chapman was a member of the LeConte party. Her diary entry for Saturday, July 6, 1901, is as follows:

The rough pine box covered with green boughs of his beloved trees has just passed from among us & the grandeur of these mountains he loved reverently. Dr. LeConte the great, the friend of all that is best in the human heart or in nature has died this day.

Here at the base of the giant cliffs of Glacier Point with the roar of the great Yosemite his Yosemite fall in his ears, he passed away quietly, gently, this morning about ten oclock. His daughter Mrs. Davis was with him. It was that he might show her the beauties of the valley that he made this trip. He felt quite well in the early morning had his breakfast and shortly after felt pains about his heart. The Dr from the hotel Dr Cross came out and assured him it was only the effect of a slight attack of indigestion. The dear old man knew himself better and told the Dr it was his heart (calling it by the scientific name of the disease). The Dr left to return to the hotel for some heart stimulant when Mrs Davis ran from her tent calling for someone with her frightened face telling the tale of the possible sorrow.

The grand old man had gone beyond, had passed from the glorious heights of his beloved Yosemite on to the greater heights beyond. For such souls there must be greater heights. So pure so noble a human being could not perish. No, the sparks he has kindled in every heart that ever touched his life in ever so slight a way shall live forever in his praise. A light mist actually settled above the grand heights veiling the intense sun during the moment of his passing. I noted this with surprise at the time for I was walking up through the Valley from the Glacier Point trail & greeted the cool with delight little knowing what was to await me. It seemed then a fitting tribute from Nature to the giant man passing.

A heavy pall rested upon the camp. The body was carried to a sheltered tent a bit apart. A rough pine box was made from the wood of the trees he loved so tenderly and in this packed with hay the body rested for its long sad journey out of the valley. The sad party started about 4:30 leaving behind a small gathering of heart heavy men & women young & old standing with bared heads. Our one wish was that his body might rest here among these monuments of the centuries with the murmur of the trees to lull and distant roar of the cataracts to soothe the sleep of the man who dwelt upon their mysteries.

To know one such man is worth the effort of a life time. He was keenly awake to everything about him and interpreted all with his heart as well as the head. Others may accomplish great things but they show the world by their smallness of heart that they themselves are not great. Here was a man who seemed as it were unconscious of his power humble before the great works of god simple as a child. God how we shall miss him here in this world of little men here in this world of perfected nature! [*Bertha L. Chapman, "Account of a Visit to Yosemite," July, 1901.*]

Joseph LeConte's funeral ride out of the valley, the stage carrying his body for the last time past the valley's enduring monuments, Yosemite Falls, Eagle Peak, El Capitan, Cathedral Rock, and Bridal Veil Fall, provides an appropriate occasion for general reflection on the meaning of Yosemite for men and women everywhere. Why did LeConte return to Yosemite time and again throughout his life, and in his old age seek it out to say an especially important farewell? Why have thousands like him in spirit though not in reputation done the same? Writers over the past 140 years have given many answers to these questions. The reasons they most often cite provide the subject matter for the remainder of this book.

## Health and Happiness

PEOPLE HAVE REALIZED from the beginning that Yosemite is a place to renew tired bodies and depressed souls. The following call on behalf of Yosemite, published in the Southern California magazine entitled *The Arrowhead*, went out to war-weary Americans at the end of World War I:

*California's Prima Donna of Things Natural*
*Beckons Men and Women of the Busy World*
*Beyond the Granite Mountain Barrier.*

Yosemite's call rings with new charms and beckoning appeal in this year of peace-making and happy return to rational living.

With the dawn of peace and waning of war tension the great out-doors everywhere, offers rest, recreation, inspiration and health stabilization that will be sought by thousands who have been forced to forego vacation periods under stress of war. Worry and anxiety which are the greatest enemies to health and happiness loses itself with intensified association with nature in its superb manifestations.

Thousands are planning to go to some nook of the picturesque upper regions as a guest of nature for the purpose of getting that health-brown that she alone can give. Everybody needs it.

Naturally speaking, Yosemite is California's most beautiful daughter, and is wedded to the admiration of the world at large. This virgin of beauty, the prima donna of things natural, that has quickened the indulgence of world thinking when it meditates upon nature and its wealth of resources, is admirably ready and charmingly willing to join the League of Nations that guarantee its right to reign in human consciousness as the personification of power and glory of natureocracy. This fair daughter, Yosemite, whose name is known wherever language is spoken, has made her robes to entertain ardent vacation delegates from all corners of the earth. [*The Arrowhead (June, 1919) 7, 9.*]

Yosemite works its miraculous cures by means of two inorganic compounds in its medicine chest, air and water. The above passage continues:

The fact that our present population lives in the lower regions where the temperatures are, more or less, stable, makes climatic conditions of the higher regions a necessity for health medium. The lower plain and valley levels do not provide sufficient change in atmospheric temperature to stimulate and maintain health through protracted years of residence. Just as the oak needs the cold to stimulate its leaf-shedding processes and the following sap-rising, so the human organisms demand atmospheric changes to recharge the human body. Two weeks in a mountain snow zone will give better tonic than anything procurable in lower regions. They are nature's own health gardens.

Doubtless there is no gift of the higher altitude that is more conducive to recharging human organisms than the snow-pure pine ozoned breeze. The very nature of negotiating via the foot route the trails that lead up and up, requires heavy using of the air consuming organs, therefore immediate and impelling use of this breath from nature. It isn't the pedal effort that causes fast breathing in higher altitudes, it's the lightness of the air. It's the kind of air that talks plain horse-sense to the breather—it lubricates, refines, purifes and charges the blood corpuscles in a refinery that is known to possess corrective properties of great value.

H-2-O, the human radiator liquid of the interior sections of the state is often tinctured with alkali or other minerals that more or less incapacitate the human water system. The water supply of today in the high mountains was snow or ice yesterday. Impurities break down under the freezing and re-freezing processes through which the water passes in its slow filtering journey from the snow zone. Taking "one" on nature in the land of snow is a privilege that is rated highly by those who know the mountains. Microbats, etc., cannot survive the board of health precautions of the high out doors. The change of water is as desirable and helpful as the change of air and the two combined are twin first aids that add glow and zest to human organisms. [*9-11.*]

Galen Clark postulated an ingenious if highly improbable physiology to account for the salutary effects of Yosemite air:

We need no blue glass Sanitarium here. The atmosphere is so pure and clear, that the sky is of a very intense blue, and seems a low arched cerulean vault above, resting upon the high walls and peaks around the valley. It is a great luxury to breathe this pure mountain atmosphere. It exhilarates and thrills through every nervous fibre of the body, and makes the old feel young again. THE BRAIN BREATHES AS WELL AS THE LUNGS! The lungs inhale atmospheric *air*, the brain *electricity*. As the air rushes through the nostrils on its way to inflate the lungs, the brain attracts and inhales electricity from it. Perhaps this is one of our old mother Nature's secrets, that many have not found out, but everyone who has been two hours in a close lecture-room or theater, has felt the immediate reviving effects of it, as soon as they had inhaled one breath on reaching the open air. Hence the great importance for many reasons, why we should breathe through the nose instead of the mouth. I have found that by perseverance in breathing through the nose, that I could climb mountains with much less fatigue than when I went *panting* with my mouth open half of the time. The reason is that the *brain* is better supplied with *nerve power*. [*Galen Clark, "Yosemite Valley, Its Wondrous Beauties" (1879) 30.*]

William Doxey in his *Guide to San Francisco and the Pleasure Resorts of California* (1897) summed up the case for Yosemite:

The Yosemite is the climax of California's incomparable mountain scenery. "See Paris and die," is the old adage. "See Yosemite and live," is the revised version. Life is richer, fuller, more comprehensive forever after. [192.]

## *Freedom*

AS YOSEMITE AIR AND WATER dissolve and carry away the contaminants of civilization, the spirit is released from the bondage of worry and care. It feels an exhilarated sense of freedom, so in keeping with the mood of the American West:

Few of us indeed are so well adapted to modern conditions of living that Nature's call to play Gypsy a while finds no response. There comes a longing to revert to the natural ways of living our early ancestors enjoyed, and to throw off for a time some of the shackles with which civilization has bound us. [*Raymond H. Bailey, "Camping and Mountaineering in Yosemite National Park" (1921) 271.*]

The father of Yosemite freedom is John Muir, who responded so passionately to the call of the Yosemite wild:

Through a meadow opening in the pine woods I see snowy peaks about the headwaters of the Merced above Yosemite. How near they seem and how clear their outlines on the blue air, or rather in the blue air; for they seem to be saturated with it. How consuming strong the invitation they extend! Shall I be allowed to go to them? Night and day I'll pray that I may, but it seems too good to be true. Some one worthy will go, able for the Godful work, yet as far as I can I must drift about these love-monument mountains, glad to be a servant of servants in so holy a wilderness. [*Muir*, MY FIRST SUMMER *(1911) 16.*]

Another glorious Sierra day in which one seems to be dissolved and absorbed and sent pulsing onward we know not where. Life seems neither long nor short, and we take no more heed to save time or make haste than do the trees and stars. This is true freedom, a good practical sort of immortality. Yonder rises another white skyland. How sharply the yellow pine spires and the palm-like crowns of the sugar pines are outlined on its smooth white domes. And hark! the grand thunder billows booming, rolling from ridge to ridge, followed by the faithful shower. [*39.*]

## *Humility*

HUMAN BEINGS have a strong need to associate with something greater by far than themselves. Initially they feel small in the presence of objects so colossal and durable:

> Here amid the deafening, roaring sound of the mighty waters of Yosemite Falls as they came rushing down from the upper world, and, with perpendicular cliffs of granite rising hundreds of feet still higher than the great falls, and looking as if they were just ready to fall over and bury us beneath their terrible immensity, man feels his utter insignificance, as he can feel it nowhere else on earth. [*S. H. West*, LIFE AND TIMES OF S. H. WEST *(1908) 81-82.*]

So humbled by hugeness, they are able to put themselves in the proper perspective:

> There is but one spot on El Capitan's upper margin where one can lie down and look into the abyss, 3,300 feet beneath him. If a man is a little touched with self-conceit, let him seek this position, or at its base place his back against the 3,300 feet wall of solid granite. Then in his humility and thankfulness would he exclaim with good old Job, "What is man that thou shouldst magnify him." [*James Mason Hutchings, "The Yosemite Valley" (1876) 25.*]

But, curiously enough, feeling little is not belittling. Gaining a true perspective on the human self in the presence of great natural objects is enabling and ennobling:

In the course of human events, it became our happy privilege to be banded together as campers, to visit collectively, and inspect individually, the glorious beauties and sublime effects of the world-renowned Yo Semite. We have come, we have seen, and have we conquered? Yea, verily we have. You ask what? We have conquered our conceit of self, and feel the majesty of the everlasting rocks, the silent awe of snow-capped mountains, the wild reckless rush of cascade, and the magnificent fall of water. [*Marcia D. Crane*, ARCADIA AND THE LION'S DEN. CAMPING PARTY TO YO SEMITE, JUNE 1886, 3.]

In addition, American citizens find that humility promotes the democratic spirit. From a natural perspective we are all equal:

We made our home at one of the great camps, while in the valley, and it was surely a place where democracy prevailed. The idea that one is better than another is only because we don't fully appreciate what mere microbes we are on this earth and have nothing really to be stuck up about. Democracy in the Yosemite is not strange. Trees eight thousand years old, rocks so huge it would take hundreds of man-built skyscrapers to make a shadow on them and heights and depths so great that even a city of people would make no mark upon the landscape! [*McKinney*, SEEING CALIFORNIA WITH HENERY *(1920)* 9.]

## *Secrets at the Heart of the Universe*

IT IS YOSEMITE'S ASSOCIATION with the ultimate that accounts, in the final analysis, for its extraordinary power in human affairs. We have already seen in Chapter One that the most common metaphors for Yosemite are religious. Not only is it God's temple, but its stupendous domes and mighty waters share the very attributes of God. Nevertheless, what makes a place sacred is not solely its appearance, for many ordinary-looking spots on earth are uncommonly powerful. The crucial factor is the connection it makes between the human and the more-than-human, the access it grants to the kind of spiritual forces that promote human emotional well-being. Yosemite is such a place.

At the beginning of this chapter we saw that Yosemite enters not only the imagination but the heart of those who love it. An opposite and equal entrance also takes place: its lovers are allowed entrance to its heart. When people enter there, miraculously they find themselves at the heart of earth, at the heart even of the universe itself, and can listen to its secrets:

The great rocks of Yosemite, expressing qualities of timeless, yet intimate grandeur, are the most compelling formation of their kind. We should not casually pass them by for they are the very heart of the earth speaking to us. [*Ansel Adams*, MY CAMERA IN YOSEMITE *(1949)*.]

The spell of silence was flung o'er stream and hill, and we appeared like intruders into the realm of Nature's secret repose. In contemplating the grandeur of the scene, the imagination recoils back upon itself, content to follow the reach of vision, completely paralyzed by the magnitude of the expanding vista. [*Baer, "A Trip to the Yosemite Falls" (1856).*]

How shall I describe our first day's wonderment! How recall those stupendous scenes! It is useless to repeat the old, threadbare commonplaces. To say that it was awe-inspiring; that with their magnitude those scenes crushed us down to earth, or even to tell how at last they worked the opposite effect; how the spirit was stirred within us, and asserted its superiority over mere earthly scenes, refused to be "cabin'd, cribb'd, confin'd" by any barrier line however vast. Yet such I must state is the truth; at first we were humiliated, and then exalted. At first we bowed down before the majesty of Nature's handwork, and at last it served only as a threshold through which the mind escaped, to plunge into space beyond its utmost rims of distance. [*Lambourne,* PINE BRANCHES AND SEA WEEDS *(1889) 47.*]

The measureless, inclosing walls, with these leaning towers and many other turrets all burst upon me at once. Nature had lifted her curtain to reveal the vast and the infinite. It elicited no adjectives, no exclamations. With bewildering sense of divine power and human littleness, I could only gaze in silence, till the view strained my brain and pained my eyes, compelling me to turn away and rest from its oppressive magnitude. [*Richardson,* BEYOND THE MISSISSIPPI *(1867) 421-422.*]

Ah Yosemite! Thy heart holds the secret of the Universe. In spite of ourselves we are stilled by the spirit of grandeur and greatness, until the thrill of the pulse of the Universe is felt and appreciated. [*Morse,* YOSEMITE AS I SAW IT *(1896) 7, 25.*]

# BIBLIOGRAPHIC INDEX

*Note:* In this book, pages on which authors are quoted are listed within brackets at the end of each bibliographic entry.

ADAMS, ANSEL. *My Camera in Yosemite.* Boston: Houghton Mifflin, 1949. [93]

AFLALO, F. G. *Sunset Playgrounds: Fishing Days and Others in California and Canada.* London: Hitherby & Co., 1909. [85]

*Arrowhead, The.* Los Angeles: San Pedro, Los Angeles, and Salt Lake Railroad, June, 1919. [89-90]

BAER, WILLIAM. "A Trip to the Yosemite Falls." *Mariposa Democrat,* August 5, 1856. Reprinted as "Early Days in Yosemite." *California Historical Society Quarterly* 1 (1922-23) 271-295. [58, 69-70, 94]

BAILEY, RAYMOND H. "Camping and Mountaineering in Yosemite National Park." In Ansel F. Hall, *Handbook of Yosemite National Park.* New York: Putnam, 1921. [91]

BANCROFT'S TOURIST GUIDE. *Yosemite, San Francisco and Around the Bay (South).* San Francisco: A. L. Bancroft, 1871. [13, 81]

BEADLE, J. H. *The Undeveloped West; or Five Years in the Territories.* Philadelphia: National Publishing Co., 1873. [37]

BEAUVOIR, LUDOVIC MARQUIS DE. *Pekin, Jeddo, and San Francisco: The Conclusion of a Voyage Round the World.* London: John Murray, 1872. [37, 82]

BICKNESS, EDMUND, compiler. *Ralph's Scrap Book.* Lawrence, MA: The Andover Press, 1905. [38]

"Bound for Yosemite." Diary of an 1896 trip to Yosemite. Madera County Historical Society. [61]

BOWLES, SAMUEL. *Across the Continent.* Springfield, MA: Samuel Bowles & Co., 1866. [35]

BRYANT, HAROLD C. "Methods of Nature Guiding." *Yosemite Ranger-Naturalist Manual* (Washington, D.C.: United States Department of the Interior, National Park Service, Second edition, 1929) 28-35. [52]

BUNNELL, LAFAYETTE HOUGHTON. *Discovery of the Yosemite, and the Indian War of 1851 Which Led to That Event.* Chicago: Fleming H. Revell, 1880. [19-21]

CAMMERER, ARNO B. "The National Parks, Our Outdoor Classrooms." *The Far Western Travelers' Annual* (1923) 47-53. [49-50]

CARR, CLARK EZRA. *My Day and Generation.* Chicago: A. C. McClurg & Co., 1908. [30]

CHAPMAN, BERTHA L. "Account of a Visit to Yosemite." Diary, July, 1901. Yosemite Collection. [88-89]

CLARK, GALEN. "Yosemite Valley, Its Wondrous Beauties." *California Farmer* 49 (1879) 30. [91]

COFFIN, CHARLES CARLETON. *Our New Way Round the World.* London: Sampson, Low, Son, and Marston, 1869. [35, 73]

CONE, MARY. *Two Years in California.* Chicago: Griggs, 1876. [32-35]

CONWAY, JOHN. "Letter from Yo Semite." *Mariposa Gazette,* April 17, 1874. [70]

CONWAY, JOHN. *Tourists' Guide from the Yosemite Valley to Eagle Peak*. San Francisco: C. W. Nevin, 1881. [61]

CRANE, MARCIA D. *Arcadia and the Lion's Den. Camping Party to Yo Semite, June, 1886*. Yosemite Collection. [93]

DAVIDSON, HANNAH AMELIA NOYES. "Nannie's Description of Yosemite Valley." 1885. Yosemite Collection. [63, 75, 78]

DODD, DERRICK. (See Frank Harrison Gassaway.)

DOXEY, WILLIAM. *Doxey's Guide to San Francisco and the Pleasure Resorts of California*. San Francisco: William Doxey, 1897. [30, 91]

ERRINGTON, HARRIET. *Letters and Journal from California 1864-65*. Yosemite Collection. [85]

GASSAWAY, FRANK HARRISON (Pseud. Derrick Dodd). *Summer Saunterings*. San Francisco: Valentine & Co., 1882. [42, 70]

GOLDSTEIN, MILTON. *The Magnificent West: Yosemite*. New York: Doubleday, 1973. [32, 57]

GREELEY, HORACE. *New York Tribune*, September 24, 1859. [41, 58]

GREENWOOD, GRACE. (See Sara Jane Clark Lippincott.)

HAIGHT, SARAH (Mrs. Edward Tompkins). Diary, May 20, 1858. Bancroft Library. [40]

HITTELL, JOHN S. *Bancroft's Pacific Coast Guide Book*. San Francisco: A. L. Bancroft & Co., 1882. [81]

HUNT, RICHARD C. "California Letters." *Democratic Banner*, Mount Vernon, Ohio, July 16–October 3, 1893. Yosemite Collection. [38, 58]

HUNT, Rev. Dr., Sermon, Yosemite Valley, August, 1871. Quoted in Alice Van Schaack, *A Familiar Letter from a Daughter to her Mother describing a few days spent at the Big Trees and the Yosemite* (Chicago: Horton & Leonard, 1871). [35]

HUTCHINGS, JAMES MASON. "The Yosemite Valley: Its Amazing Scenic Grandeur." In *The Centennial Spirit of the Times*, (July 4, 1876) 25. [92]

HUTCHINGS, JAMES MASON. Probable author of an article in *Yo Semite Assembly*, Number 1, San Francisco, August, 1877. [67]

HUTCHINGS, JAMES MASON. *In the Heart of the Sierras: The Yosemite Valley, Both Historical and Descriptive; and Scenes by the Way*. Old House, Yo Semite Valley and Oakland: Pacific Press House, 1886. [22, 69]

HUTCHINGS, JAMES MASON. "The Great Yo-Semite Valley." *Hutchings California Magazine* 4 (1859-60) 145-160, 193-208, 241-252, 385-395. [22-24, 70]

HUTCHINSON, J. S. Letter to his father, June 7, 1857. Yosemite Collection. [38]

J. W. O. "Yo-Semite." *Tuolumne Courier*, Columbia, California, July 31, 1858. [40]

JACKSON, HELEN HUNT. *Ah-wah-ne Days. A Visit to the Yosemite Valley in 1872*. San Francisco: Book Club of California, 1971. Reprinting of articles in the *New York Independent*, October 3-November 21, 1872, which are also reprinted in *Bits of Travel at Home* (Boston: Roberts Brothers, 1894). [58, 76]

JAMES, GEORGE WHARTON. *California Romantic and Beautiful*. Boston: Page Co., 1914. [57, 79]

JUMP, HERBERT ATCHINSON. *The Yosemite: a Spiritual Interpretation*. Boston: The Pilgrim Press, 1916. [63-64]

KING, CLARENCE. *Mountaineering in the Sierra Nevada*. Boston: James R. Osgood & Co., 1872. [61]

KING, THOMAS STARR. "A Vacation among the Sierras." *Boston Evening Transcript*. Scattered issues between December 1, 1860 and February 9, 1861. Reprinted by the Book Club of California. Edited by John Hussey (San Francisco, 1962). [82]

LAMBOURNE, ALFRED. *Pine Branches and Sea Weeds*. Salt Lake City, 1889. [83-84, 94]

LAWRENCE, JAMES H. "Discovery of the Nevada Fall." *Overland Monthly*. Second Series 4 (1884) 360-371. [61]

LeConte, Joseph. *The Autobiography of Joseph LeConte*. New York: Appleton & Co., 1903. [87]

LeConte, Joseph. *A Journal of Ramblings Through the High Sierras of California by the University Excursion Party*. San Francisco: Francis & Valentine, 1875. [71, 78]

*Legends of the Yosemite Miwok*. Compiled by Frank La Pena and Craig D. Bates. Illustrated by Harry Fonseca. Yosemite: Yosemite Natural History Association, 1981. [56-57]

Lehmer, O. W. *Yosemite National Park*. Chicago: Poole Brothers, printers, 1912. [14, 32]

Leland, Lilian. *Traveling Alone: A Woman's Journey around the World*. New York: American News Co., 1890. [82-83]

Lester, John Erastus. *The Atlantic to the Pacific. What to See and How to See It*. Boston: Shepard & Gill, 1873. [32]

Letchworth, Josiah. Letter to Mrs. Delia Skinner, Yosemite Valley, May 22, 1880. Yosemite Collection. [31]

Lippincott, Sara Jane Clark. (Pseud. Grace Greenwood). *New Life in New Lands: Notes of Travel*. New York: J. B. Ford & Co., 1873. [40-41, 79]

Logan, Olive. "Does It Pay to Visit Yo Semite?" *Galaxy Magazine* (October, 1870) 498-509. [47-48]

Ludlow, Fitz Hugh. "Seven Weeks in the Great Yo-Semite." *Atlantic Monthly* 13 (1864) 739-754. [24-25, 55]

Maier, Herbert. "The Purpose of the Museum in the National Parks." *Yosemite Nature Notes* 5 (1926) 37-40. [52-53]

Mast, Rev. Isaac. *The Gun, Rod and Saddle; or, Nine Months in California*. Philadelphia: Methodist Episcopal Book and Publishing House, 1875. [39]

McKinney, Dwight F. *Seeing California with Henery*. Los Angeles: Daily Doings Publishing Co., 1920. [82, 93]

"Merced—The Alf of YoSemite." *Mariposa Gazette*, June 1, 1867. [31-32]

Minturn, William. *Travels West*. London: Samuel Tinsley & Co., 1878. [78]

Moore, Ruth. "Tracks and Trails." *Yosemite School of Field Natural History*. Yearbook (1934) 163-164. [53]

Morse, Cora A. *Yosemite As I Saw It*. San Francisco: San Francisco News Co., 1896. [30, 38, 94]

Muir, John. *My First Summer in the Sierra*. Boston: Houghton Mifflin, 1911. [25-26, 55-56, 73, 92]

Paden, William G. *Seeing California*. New York: Macmillan, 1926. [82]

Pfeiffer, Emily. *Flying Leaves from East and West*. London: Field and Tuer, 1885. [83]

Plumb, Stanley. *Four Seasons in Yosemite National Park. A Photographic Story of Yosemite's Spectacular Scenery*. Photographs by Ansel Adams. Los Angeles: The Times Mirror Printing and Binding House, for Yosemite Park and Curry Co., 1936. [67]

Powell, John J. *Wonders of the Sierra Nevada*. San Francisco: Crocker, 1881. [31]

Rice, William S. "A Yosemite Valley Reminiscence." Manuscript, Yosemite Collection. [87-88]

Richardson, Albert D. *Beyond the Mississippi*. Hartford: American Publishing Co., 1867. [57, 61, 75, 94]

Ridinghood. *San Francisco Chronicle*, July 20, 1879. [78]

Robinson, Charles Dorman. "Painting a Yosemite Panorama." *Overland Monthly* New Series 22 (1893) 243-256. [14]

Robinson, Charles Dorman. *The Wawona Hotel: An Illustrated Sketch of the Sights and Scenes around the Mariposa Big Trees*. Bancroft Library. [36-37]

ROMBOLD, CHARLES C. *The National Park Experience: Normative and Interpretative Perspectives.* Dissertation, University of California, Davis, 1981. [15]

ROSS, WILLIAM WILSON. *10,000 Miles by Land and Sea.* Toronto: James Campbell & Son, 1876. [71]

SIMPSON, WILLIAM. *Meeting the Sun: A Journey All Round the World.* London: Longmans, Green, Reader, & Dyer, 1874. [29, 85]

SNYDER, GARY. "Yosemite Falls." In *Conjunctions* I and II (Double Issue). James Laughlin Festschrift. Edited by Bradford Morrow. Winter, 1981-82. [73-74]

STODDARD, CHARLES AUGUSTUS. *Beyond the Rockies: A Spring Journey in California.* New York: Scribner's Sons, 1894. [84-85]

STODDARD, CHARLES WARREN. *Poems.* San Francisco: A. Roman & Co., 1867. [72]

SYMMES, HAROLD. *Songs of Yosemite.* San Francisco: Blair-Murdock Co., 1911. [72]

TALMAGE, T. DE WITT. Sermon. Quoted in *That Wonderful Country: California for Profit and Pleasure* (San Francisco: California View Publishing Co., 1890). [79, 84]

WEBB, WILLIAM SEWARD. *California and Alaska.* New York: Putnam's Sons, 1890. [29]

WEST, S. H. *Life and Times of S. H. West.* Leroy, Illinois: S. H. West, 1908. [92]

WHITE, STEWART EDWARD. *The Mountains.* Garden City, New York: Doubleday, Page & Co., 1920. [42-47]

WHITNEY, J. D. *The Yosemite Book.* New York: Julius Bien, 1868. [57]

WILSON, HERBERT EARL. *The Lore and the Lure of Yosemite.* Los Angeles: Wolfer Printing Co., 1928. [14, 37, 38, 62, 63]

YARD, ROBERT STERLING. *The Book of the National Parks.* New York: Scribner's, 1919. [49]

YARD, ROBERT STERLING. *Top of the Continent: Story of a Cheerful Journey through our National Parks.* New York: Scribner's, 1917. [62]

*Yosemite Nature Notes.* [49, 50-52, 52-53]

*Yosemite over Indian Trails.* June 30, 1909. Manuscript, Yosemite Collection. Given to Louise Boyd Arnold of Hemet, California, by a Mr. Hitchcock, a former minister, and possibly the author. [26-29]

"Yosemite Valley." *Mariposa Gazette*, June 29, 1867. [36]

*"Wawona," Oldest Living Thing:*
*Historical Events During Its Lifetime*, no date
Postcard
Collection, Mary Vocelka

YOSEMITE AS WE SAW IT

This book is published by the Yosemite Association
on the occasion of the 100th anniversary of Yosemite National Park.

Type composition in Sabon
by Mackenzie-Harris, San Francisco.
Printed on Mohawk Superfine paper
by Meriden-Stinehour Press, Lunenburg, Vermont.
Bindery by Acme Book Binding, Charleston, Massachusetts.
Designed by Desne Border, San Francisco.